leidos

A Kaleidoscope of Innovation:
THE STORY OF LEIDOS

A Kaleidoscope of Innovation:
THE STORY OF LEIDOS

Jeffrey L. Rodengen & Christian Ramirez

Edited by Christian Ramirez and Bonny Johnson
Design and layout by Sandy Cruz

Write Stuff
Since 1986

Write Stuff Enterprises, LLC
1001 South Andrews Avenue, Suite 200
Fort Lauderdale, FL 33316
(954) 462-6657
www.writestuff.com

The publisher has made every effort to identify and locate the source of the photographs included in this edition of *A Kaleidoscope of Innovation: The Story of Leidos*. Grateful acknowledgment is made to those who have kindly granted permission for the use of their materials in this edition. If there are instances where proper credit was not given, the publisher will gladly make any necessary corrections in subsequent printings.

Publisher's Cataloging-In-Publication Data
(Prepared by The Donohue Group, Inc.)

Names: Rodengen, Jeffrey L., author. | Ramirez, Christian, 1980– author, editor. | Johnson, Bonny, 1971– editor. | Cruz, Sandy, designer. | Beyster, Mary Ann, writer of supplementary textual content.

Title: A kaleidoscope of innovation : the story of Leidos / Jeffrey L. Rodengen and Christian Ramirez ; edited by Christian Ramirez and Bonny Johnson ; design and layout by Sandy Cruz ; [foreword by Mary Ann Beyster].

Other Titles: Story of Leidos

Description: Fort Lauderdale, FL : Write Stuff Enterprises, LLC, [2018] | Includes bibliographical references and index.

Identifiers: ISBN 9781932022988 | ISBN 9781932022995 (ebook)

Subjects: LCSH: Leidos, Inc.—History. | High technology industries—United States—History. | Technological innovations—United States—History.

Classification: LCC HC79.H53 R64 2018 (print) | LCC HC79.H53 (ebook) | DDC 338.4760973—dc23

Also by Jeffrey L. Rodengen

Please visit WriteStuff.com for a complete listing

TABLE *of* CONTENTS

FOREWORD
By Mary Ann Beyster

President, The Beyster Foundation for Enterprise Development.

Educational documentary/ multimedia producer.

Board member, Scripps Institution of Oceanography, and other nonprofits in education, conservation, and the arts.

maryannbeyster.com

T WASN'T OBVIOUS THAT MY FATHER, JOHN ROBERT "BOB" BEYSTER, would be an entrepreneur, but starting businesses was in the family's history. His great grandfather Johannes "John" Beyster was a carpenter, who in 1865 emigrated from the Netherlands. John became the founder of the Beyster Lumber Company in 1877 and a noted businessman in Detroit for his close attention to every detail of his business. Focus on business details would be a personal trait apparent three generations later as my father founded and grew Science Applications International Corporation (SAIC).

My father grew up in Detroit, at a time when Michigan had been a hotbed of innovation and industry like nowhere else in the United States. Although the Beyster Lumber Company brought some financial stability during the Depression era, he witnessed countless businesses go bankrupt.

After serving in the U.S. Navy and graduating from the University of Michigan with several degrees, including a PhD, he put his education, which was paid for through the GI Bill, to good use and began a career working at research laboratories. After developing an excellent reputation in nuclear engineering and earning a small pool of stock options at General Atomics, he decided to start Science Applications International, as it was called initially. At that time, he was 45 years old, married, and with three children—Jim, Mark, and me.

In the early days of SAIC, Bob Beyster recruited "triple threat people." These were individuals who could win, deliver, and grow the work. He envisioned technical people running the company and working with customers facing challenging technical problems. His default was to give employees a chance to be creative and innovative, while having the right safety nets for those taking calculated risks.

SAIC was not a company for the entitled. Managers needed to earn the right to keep their business area. And if things didn't work, Dr. B, as he was called, wanted to know why and what was learned to move forward. Managers were encouraged to bring issues up early. If not, there were limits on how far that individual would go in the company.

My father expected employees to take ownership of their business or jobs, and in return, he shared ownership of the company broadly. In an interview with economic sociologist Dr. Joseph Blasi, he said "it [employee ownership] came from the fundamental idea of fairness that the people who created wealth should share in that wealth." There was no doubt in my father's mind that broad-based employee ownership drove the success of the company. As a result, SAIC became an incubator of talented employees leading thousands of multimillion-dollar business units. While everyone was expected to market the company, Bob Beyster was the ultimate marketer and chief recruiter of talent at all levels in the company.

After 10 years, total revenues exceeded $150 million, and you couldn't name an advanced technology field that SAIC wasn't involved in. Continuing over the decades, employees figured out how to be a part of important developments. Many times that was starting small and quickly building momentum. Sometimes that meant taking big steps.

Many have shared with me that Dr. B would keep tabs on their careers. Those who decided to leave the company found that he'd look out for them in some way, either by encouraging business collaborations, giving job references, or helping with the adoption of employee ownership at their companies through his nonprofit Foundation for Enterprise Development and later The Beyster Institute at the University of California, San Diego.

Periodically, I hear from former employees at Leidos and SAIC, and even former customers or competitors, that when facing a difficult business or technical situation, they often step back and think: "What would Dr. B do?"

He didn't think in absolutes, especially with complex decisions. He wouldn't expect everyone or every situation to be perfect on all dimensions. For example, the right team was more important than the "perfect" organizational structure. Thus, the company had more of an organic nature—a pairing of people—to allow for new business units to form or be re-formed.

In his book, *The SAIC Solution*, he reminded us that one of his favorite posters read: "None of Us is as Smart as All of Us." My mom, Betty, gave him that poster before I was born, and it hung in his office for the rest of his life. It's a simple statement that reflected his belief that "the secret sauce behind SAIC's success is the people—the employees. It's creating an environment that allows individuals to make a difference and be recognized for it."

Later in life when reflecting on the beginnings and growth of SAIC, Dr. B stated he was "a bricklayer—I like to see something grow from nothing." Those bricks built a company for experimentation, which was a natural fit for him and his fellow entrepreneurs. He was proud of the legacy of the company and of its alumni who are leaders in industry, government, and nonprofits. He was proud of the company instilling an entrepreneurial spirit, belief in a participative culture and ownership, and passion for doing something important. These are the essential Bob Beyster bricklaying blocks. The passion for serving his country was present from the company's founding in 1969 through its first 50 years, and that same passion will be behind its success as Leidos for the next 50 years. My mother, family, and I are excited that the company's past is a basis of learning and inspiration for its future.

ACKNOWLEDGMENTS

S
EVERAL DEDICATED INDIVIDUALS ASSISTED IN THE RESEARCH, preparation, and publication of *A Kaleidoscope of Innovation: The Story of Leidos*. Research Assistants Eric Barton and Torrey Kim accomplished the principal archival research for the book. Senior Editor Bonny Johnson managed the editorial content, while Senior Vice President/Creative Services Manager Sandy Cruz brought the story to life.

We would like to extend our gratitude to Mary Ann Beyster for her foreword contribution in honor of her father and Leidos founder J. Robert Beyster. We would also like to thank Leidos Chairman and CEO Roger Krone for allowing us to tell the story of this innovative company that continues to develop solutions that make the world safer, healthier, and more efficient.

Special gratitude goes to Melissa Koskovich, Ryan Fisher, Michelle Wagner, and Michelle Maffeo, who helped shepherd this book to completion and whose considerable time and collaborative efforts provided invaluable guidance to the storytelling process.

We would also like to thank past and present Leidos partners, employees, retirees, and friends who were generous with their time and insights. We are particularly beholden to those whose thoughts and words added important historical context to the story, including: Ann Addison, Brian Anderson,

Patrick Bannister, Sondra Barbour, Doug Barton, Edouard Benjamin, Mary Ann Beyster, Betty Bidwell, Michele Brown, Jim Cantor, Nevin Carr, Michael Chagnon, Paul Coakley, Michael Coogan, Rus Cook, Stuart Crawford, Charles Croom, Mike Daniels, Kim Denver, Gerry Fasano, Chuck Fralick, John Fratamico, Bob Gemmill, James Grant, Walter Harris, Walt Havenstein, Charles Heflebower, Angela Heise, Jerald Howe, Ravi Hubbly, Steve Hull, Fay Hung, Bobby Ray Inman, Deborah Lee James, Anita Jones, Donna Jones, John Jumper, Brian Keller, Frank Kendall, William Krampf, Bill Kraus, Tony Leiter, Doug Lowy, Vince Maffeo, Jim Moos, Tony Ng, Arnold Punaro, James Reagan, Tim Reardon, Robert Rosenberg, Jim Russell, Jonathan Scholl, James Shiflett, Ralph Sievers, Mark Sopp, Gloria Spikes, Ray Veldman, Daniel Voce, Doug Wagoner, George Walther-Meade, Sharon Watts, Bettina Garcia Welsh, and Ron Zollars.

Finally, special thanks are extended to the staff at Write Stuff Enterprises, LLC, who worked diligently and tirelessly to produce this book: Kim Campbell, managing editor; Cristofer Valle, graphic designer and studio administrator; Ligia Leonardi, graphic designer; Sarah Alender, Connie Greenawald, Christine McIntire, Laurie Russo, and Sharon Tripp, proofreaders; Lisa Ryan, indexer; Amy Major, executive assistant to Jeffrey L. Rodengen; Marianne Roberts, president, publisher, and chief financial officer; and Tiffany Massenburg, marketing assistant.

CHAPTER ONE

IT STARTED WITH SCIENCE

At one time, years ago, I might have been voted by my coworkers as someone 'least likely to start up his own business.' A nuclear physicist by trade, I was first and foremost a scientist, not an entrepreneur.

———————————

J. Robert Beyster, PhD
COMPANY FOUNDER

J. Robert Beyster, PhD, wasn't unhappy working as a nuclear physicist and chairman of the Accelerator Physics Department at San Diego's General Atomics, but he had a notion that he might be able to make a living with his own firm. He certainly did not envision founding what would eventually become a $10 billion Fortune 500 company. He was simply interested in finding, as he described: "A good place where I could work and maybe a few people could join me, so I could continue to live in San Diego and keep my wife happy."

Beyster's hope was to find talented scientists and engineers who wanted to contribute to developing scientific solutions to issues that were important to the country. He also believed it was important to create a company built on a foundation of employee ownership and a culture of entrepreneurship. He would do just that. In 1969, Science Applications Incorporated (SAI) was born.

The following year, the company posted its first profits when the 20-employee firm brought in $243,000 in revenue, thanks in part to its first long-term client, the Defense Atomic Support Agency (DASA). Beyster's simple idea transformed not only his career, but the lives of people all over the world. SAI's early days were the impetus for global innovations that have made the world a better and safer place to live.

Opposite: Science Applications Incorporated's (SAI) first office was in La Jolla, California. SAI paid just $2.40 per square foot annually for the space, which boasted a view of the Pacific Ocean.

J. Robert Beyster (third row from bottom, far left) enlisted in the U.S. Navy after graduating high school. *(Photo from the SAIC collection, University of California San Diego.)*

A Solid Foundation

Before John Robert Beyster became the pioneering founder of one of the United States' largest government contracting firms, he was a young boy who was taught hard work and commitment. Beyster learned these lessons watching his family survive the Great Depression, and he developed his undying sense of corporate loyalty from hearing his father discuss his career at General Motors.

Born in 1924 in Detroit and raised in nearby Grosse Ile, Beyster started his post-high school career by joining the Navy, where he served on a destroyer during World War II. Thanks to the government's GI Bill, he subsequently graduated from the University of Michigan, where he earned several degrees, including a PhD in nuclear physics in 1950.

1924

CREDIT: PHOTO DETAIL COURTESY OF BEYSTER FAMILY.

J. Robert Beyster is born in Detroit, Michigan. His grandparents live in the rented duplex unit below him and have a substantial impact on his early life.

1929

The Great Depression grips the nation. A young Beyster watches his father persevere with help from family members. Beyster's own work ethic and negative view toward bankruptcy would be formed during this period of economic hardship.

1942

CREDIT: THE SAIC COLLECTION, UC SAN DIEGO.

Beyster (bottom left) joins the U.S. Navy, where he eventually serves on a destroyer stationed at the Naval Station Norfolk, in Norfolk, Virginia.

1950

CREDIT: THE SAIC COLLECTION, UC SAN DIEGO.

With increasing government and industrial interest and research in nuclear energy, Beyster (center) earns a PhD in nuclear physics from the University of Michigan.

Beyster settled into a career at the Los Alamos National Laboratory for 5 years, followed by 12 years at General Atomics, where he headed up the accelerator physics department. When Gulf Oil acquired General Atomics in the 1960s, Beyster felt that the senior management held little interest in the research that his department was performing, so he cashed out some of his General Atomics stock and used the proceeds as seed money to launch his own firm.

Above: Beyster (center) graduated from the University of Michigan and later returned to earn a PhD in nuclear physics. *(Photo from the SAIC collection, University of California San Diego.)*

Left: Beyster and Gene Haddad at the General Atomics linear accelerator (LINAC).

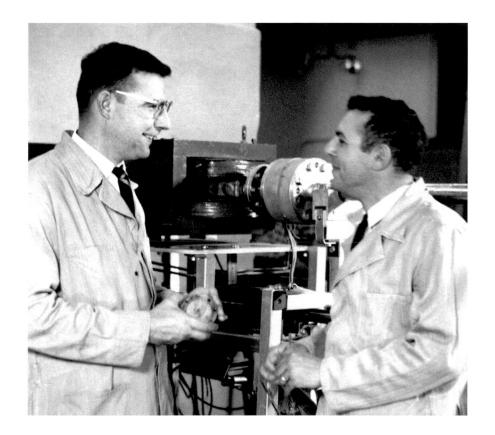

1968

Beyster cashes out some of his General Atomics stock and decides to start his own firm "to perform research in a productive environment."

1968

While still in the planning stages of the start-up, Beyster commits to having an employee-owned company, which he believes will help promote stability.

1969

FEBRUARY 3

At the age of 45, with a wife and three kids to support, Beyster takes the leap and officially launches his new company—Science Applications Incorporated (SAI).

1969

Beyster invests $50,000 of his own assets and secures a bank loan using his family home as collateral to launch the new firm in La Jolla, California.

Betty Beyster gave her husband Bob this poster to put up in his new office in 1969.

The Business Plan

Instead of creating a fancy business plan, Beyster's first planning session for his upstart company was to create a list called "things to do," on which the first item was "pick a name and letterhead." After mulling over several names, including San Diego Research Associates, Trigon, Kepler, and Rutherford Research Corporation, Beyster and his associates settled on Science Applications Incorporated. They felt the name encompassed everything the new business would handle, but it was also simple and not overly grandiose.

Beyster handwrote an organizational plan in 1968 that said the company's goal was "to perform research in a productive environment." At the center of that environment was the company's most important, legendary hallmark—its commitment to employee ownership.

"The company was often referred to as Bob Beyster's company," noted Mary Ann Beyster—the founder's daughter. "He would take offense to that. He expected and wanted to inspire people to act like it was their own company, and that's exactly what they did."

Beyster made it a priority to ensure all of his staff members owned a portion of the company, and he used employee ownership as a recruitment and retention strategy to build SAI. Patrick Bannister, a research analyst with the company, recalled:

1969

SAI hires computer specialist and former fellow General Atomics employee Don Huffman as one of its first three employees.

1969

SAI lands its first contract, a $70,000 project for the Defense Atomic Support Agency, researching nuclear weapons' output, along with technical consulting contracts from the Atomic Energy Commission and Los Alamos National Laboratory.

1969

Beyster decides to use his own staff members as SAI's frontline sales and marketing team.

1969

Fledgling firm SAI earns $20,000 during its first year in business, which comes as such a surprise to Beyster that he assumes he made an accounting error.

SCIENTISTS AS SALES STAFF

The company's earliest scientists were also responsible for selling SAI's services, allowing them to develop close customer relationships and cut down on expenses. New employees quickly learned that they had to play a part in the company's growth and profitability. Some excelled at selling new work, while others showed talent for presentations, but each person eventually found his or her place. "Everybody had to learn to become a marketing agent for the company," said Matt Tobriner, a longtime SAIC employee and board member. "And if you weren't good at that, as long as you found someone within SAI who was willing to keep you alive and feed you work, that was fine, but even these people were expected to help write proposals and get in front of the customer and represent the company outside the work environment."

Beyster's decision to put the company's most valuable minds on the front lines of marketing and sales pitches turned out to be a stroke of genius, and the policy endured throughout the years.

"How we go about our marketing is one of the most important considerations for the future of SAI," Beyster wrote in 1983. "Successful marketing is built upon the reputation of the company and our technical staff for performing superior and, in some cases, unique technical work. Since the primary operating entities within SAI are the groups, most of the marketing resources should be left with the groups."

1970

By the end of the first year, SAI has grown to 20 employees, with most coming from General Atomics.

1970

SAI ends the fiscal year with $243,000 in revenue.

1970

A study of radiation-based cancer therapy for the Los Alamos National Laboratory sparks the company's health business.

1971

SAI launches its Technology Systems Group in the Washington, D.C., region to study data from nuclear weapon dust clouds.

These guys [employees] all, for the most part, had PhDs and were recognized in their field and all that type of stuff, but there was another element of an entrepreneurial overachieving aspect of them. People worked very hard. They wanted stock. They wanted options.

Every employee had goals and everyone was an overachiever. "It was learned fairly quickly that every person had a role in growing the business and making the business profitable," explained Mary Ann Beyster.

In his past positions, Beyster had watched colleagues leave the companies that employed them, using the knowledge and ideas they had gleaned from those employers to start their own companies. They would then nurture their firms so they could sell them and move on to their next entrepreneurial ventures. That was never Beyster's goal.

Beyster was not creating a business to become wealthy. He wanted to create a stable environment where professional people had the opportunity to perform superior scientific and technical work, while still having a say in policies and the management of the company. Though employees were exposed to a minimal number of distracting outside influences and pressures that come with employee ownership, they would be fairly rewarded with recognition and financial compensation for doing good work.

In his 1983 document "Some Principles and Practices of SAI," Beyster said, "It is not a get-rich-quick organization or a high-roller speculative organization. It is an organization where the long-term and short-term rewards are expected to be fair to all."

As SAI grew, those rewards turned out to be more than fair.

In the mid-1970s, SAI's employees presented Beyster with this cartoon, humorously illustrating his attempt to steer the company's fiercely independent "entrepreneurs" in one direction. *(Illustration courtesy of J. Robert "Bob" Beyster Estate.)*

EMPLOYEE OWNERSHIP

When J. Robert Beyster, PhD, launched Science Applications Incorporated in 1969, he was slightly uncomfortable with the idea of starting a business, because it suggested that he was abandoning his scientific pursuits. Therefore, he launched the firm as an employee-owned business. "I didn't read it from anybody," he later said about the idea. "I did it that way because I thought it was right."

His holdings in the company were reduced from 100 percent in the early days to just 10 percent by the end of the company's first year in business. Beyster became a champion for employee ownership as a competitive advantage and as a way to attract top talent.

"In keeping with our 'employee ownership' philosophy, SAI is presently a non-public company," Beyster wrote in 1983. "The basic premise of the SAI stock policy is that those who contribute to the company should own it and that ownership should be based on that contribution and performance as much as feasible. External, disinterested individuals who would own part of the company and contribute little do not deserve to benefit by the hard work of the individuals within the company."

Forbes magazine profiled Beyster in a cover story in 1997, by which point, Beyster's stock was worth about $27 million—but would have been worth about $2 billion if he had maintained all of it rather than sharing it with employees— and he had no regrets. The company made millionaires out of hundreds of employees, and Beyster set up the Foundation for Enterprise Development to help other businesses implement similar employee-ownership programs.

"Beysterism is spreading," *Forbes* wrote, noting an uptick in companies offering stock to employees. "What are these companies finding? That sharing the wealth with their workers works wonders."

In the Black

Unlike many start-ups, SAI did not obtain investments from private equity or venture capital. Instead, Beyster invested $50,000 of his own money and secured a bank loan with his home as collateral. Beyster was able to pay his employees' salaries with that funding, even though he deferred his own salary for the company's first year of business.

At the beginning, Beyster was joined by just one employee, Don Huffman, a computer specialist. The timing of SAI's launch coincided with the U.S. government's decision to stop performing atmospheric testing of nuclear weapons, and one of Beyster's areas of interest was simulating nuclear outcomes with the use of accelerators. Fortuitously, SAI's first contract was a $70,000 job with DASA, researching nuclear weapons' output. Not long thereafter, SAI also won contracts with the Atomic Energy Commission and the Los Alamos National Laboratory. SAI's expertise in the nuclear field would continue to pay off in the future.

Former employee retired Colonel Ralph Sievers, U.S. Army Corps of Engineers, who worked for the company for almost 20 years, was part of a team at Kirtland Air Force Base in Albuquerque, New Mexico. The team used a solar furnace to recreate the light intensity from a nuclear burst, melting soil test samples. "We were providing detailed types of information for the ability to predict nuclear weapon effects," explained Sievers. It was one of many successful projects launched after SAI's first year in business, a year that saw the company garner $243,000 in revenues with a $20,000 profit. SAI was in the black.

When Beyster discovered that SAI made a five-figure profit during its first year, he was so surprised that he phoned one of his board members and told him that something had to be wrong—after all, this band of researchers knew almost nothing about entrepreneurialism and income, so to see such a generous profit so quickly surely had to be a mistake.

Retired U.S. Army Corps of Engineers Colonel Ralph Sievers conducted research on the effects of nuclear weapons using the solar furnace located at Kirtland Air Force Base in Albuquerque, New Mexico.

After being assured that it was not, Beyster was encouraged to launch an initial public offering for the fledgling firm, but he remained stalwart in his belief that this was the wrong track. "Something must have happened to stop me from buying into this traditional approach," he later wrote. "I had observed that it can also destroy a company and harm all but a limited number of insiders—most often the top executives—who do very well financially."

SAI performed extensive tests and research on thermonuclear simulation and the impact of nuclear weapons on the atmosphere.

Growing Swiftly

By 1970, SAI had already filed to do business in the Commonwealth of Virginia, where the firm established a satellite office to ease the workload of government contracts. Offices in Los Angeles and Alabama quickly followed. With the company growing both in employee numbers and geographically, it was up to Beyster to ensure that SAI remained a cohesive group, even as it continued to maintain its entrepreneurial spirit. The company's employee-owned entrepreneurial business model also created internal competition and a Darwinian-like culture, which Beyster encouraged. It was a culture where the most capable, hardest-working, motivated, and mission-passionate employees who grew the company thrived, while those less capable were weeded out or put into reduced roles.

"I made sure that SAIC's organizational structure remained extremely fluid and flexible, even as the pressures of growth pushed us to make things more rigid and inflexible," he later wrote.

Striking that balance would not only be key to SAI's success, but it would also define Beyster's leadership style as the firm became larger. And no one at SAI—neither its employees nor its customers—could have guessed just how big it would grow over the coming years. ∎

CHAPTER TWO

SOLUTIONS CREATE GROWTH

Dad had a reputation of being the ultimate marketer. He marketed people. If he had identified someone that he wanted in the company or someone in the company was recruiting an individual, he was all about making sure they knew that he wanted them in.

Mary Ann Beyster
J. ROBERT BEYSTER'S DAUGHTER

A
S SCIENCE APPLICATIONS, INC., WON MORE PROJECT BIDS AND hired more employees, J. Robert Beyster saw the opportunity and the need for the firm to connect its far-reaching skills and goals into one larger, integrated company. The first step Beyster took to accomplish this integration was to change the name of the company in 1983 from SAI to Science Applications International Corporation (SAIC).

With the name change, Beyster also established several company-wide initiatives, such as a Proposal Center and SAIC University, among others. The initiatives not only helped the firm establish a cohesive team, they also allowed staff members to share ideas on customer acquisitions, problem-solving, and other important factors that helped the company grow. As the new SAIC expanded in size, it also boosted its geographic footprint to better take hold of the burgeoning need for its services.

For Beyster, company expansion was never an exercise in pride. Instead, he believed SAIC's role was to serve communities and the country by using science to solve critical problems. Beyster also believed that serving those behind the science was equally important. "He didn't have a huge ego," said Ron Zollars, Beyster's former chief of staff. "He just really cared about growing the company and making sure it was successful so, in the future, when he left, the employees would have something to be proud of."

Opposite: Science Applications International Corporation's (SAIC) emphasis on employee ownership, freedom, and entrepreneurship drew the most talented people in their respective fields to the company. *(Photo from the SAIC collection, University of California San Diego.)*

Above: J. Robert Beyster had the company name emblazoned on jackets to show that then-SAI was becoming a real team with a shared goal.

Right: The company's hierarchy of representation provided vital ideas and feedback to decision makers at Meetings Week, while engaging employees in their work and giving them a role in the decision-making process. *(Photo from the SAIC collection, University of California San Diego.)*

Surviving "Hell Week"

In the early 1970s, SAI established a quarterly Meetings Week initiative in which staff members and customers would get together, build relationships, and discuss ideas. Keeping in mind that many of the company's employees worked in different offices and some were even on-site with clients, Meetings Week provided a rare opportunity to collaborate, share ideas, and come to a consensus.

Meetings Week "was an important ingredient in the glue that kept this very decentralized organization from self-destructing," said former executive Neil Hutchinson. "It provided us with an opportunity to recognize the accomplishments of individuals from all levels of the company."

However, the week wasn't always held in such high esteem. In the early days, employees dubbed it "Hell Week" to describe the intensity of the business gatherings.

1970s

EARLY

Science Applications, Inc. (SAI), begins running its quarterly Meetings Week, where employees and customers band together, build relationships, and discuss future projects.

1972

The company employs 15 people and logs $3.3 million in revenue, with $110,852 in net income.

1972

SAI opens an office in Albuquerque to support the Air Force Weapons Laboratory. The company assists the lab with their work on electromagnetic phenomena and effects, which later becomes the foundation of the company's Physical Sciences Group.

1972

The basis for SAI's space business launches with work in space and planetary sciences in Chicago; Tucson; and Huntsville, Alabama.

Cognizant of the impact Meetings Week had and the critical role families would play in the success of Beyster's quickly growing company, his wife Betty took it upon herself to organize social events for employees' spouses. Betty's events gave the spouses an opportunity to meet, and provide one another support. Beyster's daughter Mary Ann recalled, "There were a lot of dynamics at SAIC—these gatherings helped teach spouses how to get through those and how to make the best of them."

The quarterly meetings eventually found their stride and the company created a schedule that met everyone's needs, making the event a critical part of the company's fabric.

By 1999, some 1,500 people were participating in Meetings Week, from managers to customers to select employees. During that week, the company also hosted its Management Council, where senior staff members would share details of the company's performance. Even customers would have the opportunity to hear information about the company's finances, which often surprised them, since it was not public and such transparency was rare for a private firm.

A Wide Range of Contracts

While not every decision SAI made worked out well or as envisioned, the company was able to continue its growth streak due to continued interest from private and government sources. In 1973 alone, SAI won more than 100 contracts from several sectors within the Department of Defense, making military computer systems the company's fastest-growing unit. The strength of those contracts, and others, helped more than double the firm's revenues in 1973, which rose to $21 million on the strength of its 703 employees.

Early marketing pieces, like this brochure from 1973, demonstrated then-SAI's commitment to supporting the United States' national defense efforts.

1973

CREDIT: THE SAIC COLLECTION, UC SAN DIEGO.

SAI wins more than 100 contracts from different sectors of the Department of Defense.

1973

SAI more than doubles its revenues, which rise to $21 million on the strength of its 703 staff members.

1975

Fifty-eight percent of SAI's 1,213 staff members have advanced degrees, while 87 percent hold degrees in engineering, math, or physical sciences.

1976

CREDIT: DR. ROBERT E. TURNER.

SAI logs $45.8 million in revenue, with 1,213 employees and a net income of $1.2 million.

GOING GLOBAL

SAI's first international job was with the Kuwaiti defense forces in 1976, followed by nuclear work with the U.K.'s Defense Aviation Repair Agency. In 1994, the company established a subsidiary in Mexico, SAIC de Mexico, and three years later, the firm forged a joint venture in Venezuela known as INTESA, which handled IT in Latin America.

The company's continuing track record in the international arena is surprising, considering that J. Robert Beyster almost didn't encourage it to happen. "The question for me was, why bother with international work at all?" Beyster wrote regarding his trepidation about entering the global market back in the 1970s. But he realized that it was a way to expand the company's portfolio, bring in more income, and appeal to employees, who enjoyed overseas travel.

The choice was a positive one, developing an international base that continues to this day and sends now-Leidos staff all over the world to find solutions for customers spanning the globe.

As SAI continued to grow within the United States, it was also apparent that the firm could be of great assistance on global jobs as well. In the late 1970s, SAI started working with the U.S. Navy to evaluate the feasibility of creating a command, control, and communications station for the Royal Saudi Naval Forces. The company's work on this project was so successful

1976

SAI provides technical support and management assistance to the Department of Defense's Joint Cruise Missile Program Office.

1976

SAI secures its first big global contract, which is for the Kuwaiti defense forces.

1979

SAI and the U.S. Navy join forces to determine whether it's feasible to create a command, control, and communications station for the Royal Saudi Navy.

1980

SAI plays a key role in the clean-up efforts after the nuclear accident at Three Mile Island and the contaminated Love Canal chemical dumpsite in coordination with the Environmental Protection Agency.

that it would lead to hundreds of millions of dollars in contracts with the Royal Saudi Navy.

"The Royal Saudi Naval Forces program, originally awarded in 1979, was SAI's first large international contract as well as its first large systems integration contract," Beyster later wrote. Many years after, as Beyster looked back on his long career with the company he founded, he noted that despite racking up scores of large global contracts, he always remained most proud of the Saudi contract "because it became a model of how to build a successful international relationship."

When SAI won its contract to create a command, control, and communications station for the Royal Saudi Navy in 1979, the firm was establishing its stake in the international market, where it still competes to this day.

1981

SAI sees $187.2 million in revenue, with 3,700 employees and enjoys $4.6 million in net income.

1984

SAIC®

Science Applications, Inc., changes its name to Science Applications International Corporation (SAIC).

1987

SAIC sees $599 million in revenue with 6,814 employees and logs a net income of $18 million.

1980s

LATE

J. Robert Beyster sees the field of government contracts shrinking just as the competition is growing, so he pivots the company's marketing strategy and begins submitting fixed-price contract bids for private contracts, which is a fast success.

In addition to growth via new contracts, the company was also expanding through new acquisitions. In the late 1980s, the renamed SAIC began acquiring more companies, and made its largest acquisition yet when it purchased American Systems Engineering Corporation (AMSEC). The acquisition added weight to the company's naval logistics support

A SLOGAN THAT SELLS

Since the early days of SAI, the firm's slogan was "An Employee-Owned Company," which was a business philosophy that was near and dear to J. Robert Beyster and the entrepreneurial culture of the company he founded. But as SAI grew and became SAIC, another slogan began to emerge throughout the years that perfectly described how the company had been able to convert scientific principles and skills into tailored solutions for its customers.

That slogan was "From Science to Solutions," a simple phrase that "was absolutely critical to the company's growth and ultimate success," Beyster later wrote. "I don't know of any other company that has the combination of technical skill sets as broad or deep as we did."

While the Science to Solutions way of thinking was heavily ingrained in the company's culture from the very beginning, the slogan, which became more prominent after SAIC went public, allowed the company an entry point that perfectly described its utility to potential customers. For many at SAIC, these four simple words made the job of selling and marketing the company's services, which were delivered

by the best in their respective fields, considerably easier.

Leidos Chief Technology Officer John J. Fratamico Jr., PhD, who joined SAIC in the late 1980s, explained the company's effectiveness in providing those solutions:

Fundamentally, what we excel at is the acquisition and use of information. There is a common thread across much of what we do—collecting information, optimizing the use of it, optimizing decisions based on information available—and many of our customers have what fundamentally are common problems in that regard.

Additionally, the process of applying science to solutions was always supported by a strong culture of workplace ethics, as Fratamico expressed:

You want to work for a company that's always wanting to do the right thing and always wanting to deliver a superior product to its customer, because that in the long term is what makes the most business sense.

work. AMSEC specialized in ship maintenance and engineering, which went hand in hand with SAIC's expertise in engineering.

A Genius Staff

It was always important to Beyster to ensure that his staff was comprised of subject matter experts in every area, so the company would stand out for its expertise. By 1975, 58 percent of the 1,213 staff members had advanced degrees, while some 87 percent held degrees in physical sciences, math, or engineering.

That high-level staff composition was not only the product of the expertise demanded by the work the company performed, but also thanks to Beyster's unique recruitment techniques. "My management team and I realized that if we hired the right people to begin with, the problems with having a culture of freedom would be minimized," he later wrote.

That philosophy became a self-fulfilling prophecy in the best way: Many highly educated people were seeking positions that afforded them great freedom, and Beyster wanted to give that freedom to staff members who deserved it. Therefore, the marriage of goals coincided to allow SAIC to attract the most talented staff available.

Recruiting talent: In 1974, SAI hired a research team to study electro-optics in Ann Arbor, Michigan, as a subdivision of the firm's Military Sciences Group. *(Photo courtesy of Dr. Robert E. Turner.)*

Beyster used shared ownership in the company and delegated responsibility to recruit and retain talented employees.
(Photo from the SAIC collection, University of California San Diego.)

"That's what I was after—freedom to do the work and build the work I wanted to do, in a setting that was attractive, and working with other people who were smart and motivated as entrepreneurs," said longtime executive Jim Russell. Russell's attitude has been echoed by thousands of other employees over the years who found that the freedom the company provided to its employees created the perfect setting for them to perform their scientific work at an optimum level.

Walt Havenstein, retired CEO of SAIC, described the novelty of that culture:

> I think the culture of entrepreneurship that Dr. Beyster had expected and fostered in the company made it unique. At the time, there were over a hundred business units operating in the company when I got there, and each one of those business unit general managers were very focused on their growth, satisfying their customers, and operating in an entrepreneurial way. So I think, for a company that large, that was pretty unique.

While Beyster was a brilliant scientist, it was his autonomous and entrepreneurial leadership style and his belief in empowering those individuals who brought innovative ideas to the table that ultimately earned him the most respect from his employees. "Dr. Beyster is probably the brightest guy I've ever met," said Patrick Bannister, who joined then-SAI in 1975 after working for the Environmental Protection Agency (EPA). "Not only did he know the science, but he just knew how to work with people and get the best out of people."

A Growing Powerhouse

When you think about the companies that were notable in the 1970s and 1980s, the first that come to mind are typically those that make the products we use every day: General Electric, Kellogg's, Apple, and so on. Most people would not have imagined that a firm that barely anyone had heard of—which made almost zero products—could be the powerhouse that SAIC was becoming. But the company was performing well, with significant gains every year and new contracts all the time.

By 1987, SAIC was bringing in $599 million in revenue and had 6,814 employees, logging a net income of $18 million. Yet even as the firm flourished, Beyster wasn't satisfied with maintaining the status quo, and he had the foresight to see that the business world was changing, and that SAIC would have to change with it.

One of the most important adjustments was in terms of marketing. Although SAIC had enjoyed great success securing the majority of its jobs straight from government staff, that was slowly becoming an antiquated

This image shows the SAI Board of Directors in 1974, which included (front row, left to right) W. E. Zisch, J. R. Beyster, and B. J. Shillito, as well as (back row, left to right) W. M. Layson, L. C. Fricker, and T. F. Walkowicz.

process. Other firms began to see the utility in the SAIC model and came to market hungry for a bite of the federal-contracting pie. Around the same period, the government slowed its spending, drying up some of the key income streams on which SAIC had relied on for so long. Beyster saw this sea change happening and hired a more robust financial team so the company could enter accurate, fixed-price bids for projects.

The strategy shift also capitalized on Beyster's longtime—but then-unorthodox—method of leaving contract proposals to individual teams. As SAIC managers worked with their staff to identify potential clients, departments would call upon other SAIC specialty areas for cross-disciplinary teamwork, allowing the company to pitch detail-rich, cross-sector proposals to clients that involved the expertise of a wide range of scientific minds. These complex proposals began to take hold, and the company started bringing in bigger and more robust contracts, resulting in record revenues in 1989 that rose to $865 million.

In addition to SAIC's expertise and Beyster's entrepreneurial model, it was the company's individual groups that helped set the firm apart from its competitors. Specializing in niche services, with experts from each individual area participating in projects, SAIC was ultimately able to establish itself as the broadest technical company in the industry, which it remains today as Leidos. ∎

CHAPTER THREE

CIVIL PROJECTS

The fact that we have hundreds of agencies that we provide a wide range of services to is something that is certainly a challenge. The goals are to support those unique missions by quickly adapting to the constant shifts and switches, as well as ensuring that we are providing the absolute best talent and opportunities in a way that supports our customer and also provides development.

———————

Angela L. Heise
PRESIDENT OF THE LEIDOS CIVIL BUSINESS

E VERYONE WHO HAS EVER WONDERED HOW THE AIR TRAFFIC over our skies is managed, how the International Space Station is supplied, or what it takes for bags to be screened by airport agents should be aware of the prominent role Leidos plays in these functions. From the company's early days as SAIC, civil and commercial projects were among the bread-and-butter jobs that kept scientists busy, and that is still the case today.

Leidos has become well versed in a wide variety of civil programs that keep the world operating efficiently. Through its support of U.S. cabinet-level agencies, the United Kingdom's Ministry of Defence, and commercial clients around the globe, the civil business within Leidos helps valued customers achieve their missions and citizens thrive in an increasingly complex and connected world. The company delivers trusted solutions in verticals including energy and environment, homeland security, space exploration, and transportation. But the journey to arrive at this position was one that passed through stages of emphasis on its energy, environment, and infrastructure customers.

All along the way, the company's cadre of highly specialized experts were critical to its growth and success. By creating such knowledgeable teams, Leidos has stayed on the cutting edge of civil programs, and often redraws the parameters of the possibilities in each of its areas of expertise.

Opposite: As part of its civil business, Leidos keeps the skies secure through the management of check-in and carry-on baggage screenings at more than 200 U.S. airports and as the operator of the country's air traffic control system.
(Photo by rezawikan on Visual Hunt.)

It was founder J. Robert Beyster who initially instilled the approach of pushing the boundaries in the realms of marketing, sales, and science to foster the company's growth with civilian agencies and commercial organizations. "He was our lead marketing guy, business development, and top recruiter for the company," explained Ron Zollars, who worked as Beyster's chief of staff for 10 years.

Every employee was expected to be a salesperson, to pursue new opportunities for the company, and to expand the firm's area of expertise. Managers could set their sights on just about any technical area that looked viable or customer they were interested in doing business with as long as they did not exceed their overhead. But Beyster was the lead marketing man. Much of the company's contract-building prowess was due to his uncanny ability to forge bonds with people, leading to partnerships across the globe. "From the beginning, Beyster was indefatigable, constantly on the road, promoting SAIC to any government official who would listen," *Vanity Fair* wrote. "On a 10-day trip, he'd jam in as many as 80 appointments. If he had an hour between planes, he'd order his secretary to jam in one more."

Zollars recalled travelling with Beyster:

> *If he had something in the middle of the night he was thinking of, like at eleven or twelve, he'd knock on the door and just come in and start talking. "Hey, I want you to set up a meeting with [this person] tomorrow, and by the way, we're running at five o'clock tomorrow." His mind was always racing. And he was always thinking about the next thing.*

As Beyster established himself as a scientist and salesman, he also placed special emphasis on the importance of providing excellence in

J. Robert Beyster kept a full schedule as a salesman, scientist, and chief marketer for SAIC.

1978

AUGUST

Toxic chemicals buried decades earlier begin percolating through soil in the Love Canal neighborhood near Niagara Falls in New York. SAIC supports the Environmental Protection Agency (EPA) cleanup of the contamination.

1979

CREDIT: CDC/DR. EWING.

MARCH 28

Three Mile Island nuclear station in Pennsylvania becomes the site of the worst nuclear disaster in U.S. history. SAIC plays a vital role in cleaning up the nuclear accident.

1986

After the Chernobyl disaster, SAIC is hired to assess the safety of U.S. nuclear reactor facilities. The company becomes the leading supplier of probabilistic risk assessments for the U.S. nuclear power industry.

1987

SAIC's work helping engineer the most hydrodynamic yacht for America's Cup winner *Stars and Stripes* marks one of the first times that the company receives public recognition.

customer service. He believed this could best be achieved by building close relationships with clients that would last a lifetime. For Beyster, customer service was foundational to the company's success. Staff members took note of these principles and followed suit when representing the firm to prospective clients.

Striking the perfect combination between the worlds of science, sales, and customer service would prove to be vital in building the company's civil and commercial business over the years.

Eyes on the Skies

Today, every American traveling on a private, commercial, or military aircraft puts their life in the hands of Leidos and its dedicated workforce.

In 2015, the company replaced the Federal Aviation Administration's (FAA) 40-year-old En Route host computer with the state-of-the-art satellite-based En Route Automation Modernization (ERAM) system. "Replacing the aging En Route system with ERAM was one of the most complex undertakings the FAA ever had," said Tony Ng, chief technology officer and solution architect for transportation solutions at Leidos, who added:

Imagine replacing a four-decades old system that was written in the computer language of COBOL? Imagine how hard it would be to keep maintaining it, or trying to enhance it. The system was so complex that it wasn't replaced for a long time, but it finally had to be done, so we took on the job, we won the program, and we did that deployment. We basically were tasked with replacing the heart of our national airspace system, which was the most complex piece in the FAA's modernization program called NextGen.

Angela L. Heise is president of the civil business at Leidos. She is responsible for providing solutions to U.S. cabinet-level civil agencies and major elements of the public and private sector across the globe.

1989

SAIC demonstrates the first luggage-inspection machine to pass FAA-conducted testing one year after the tragic bombing of Pan Am Flight 103 over Lockerbie, Scotland. The bomb detection device spots 95 percent of the simulated explosives during testing.

1991

SAIC forges a contract with NASA to assist with the agency's "Mission to Mars" program. It is the largest NASA win in SAIC's history up to that time, worth $150 million.

1995

SAIC acquires domain name registrar Network Solutions for $4.7 million, making it among the largest providers of Internet and e-commerce services.

1996

SAIC partners with Pinkerton, Inc., to strengthen its cybersecurity business, keeping hackers and cyber criminals at bay.

The Leidos civil business manages a large percentage of the air traffic over the United States and the world. *(Photo from PikWizard.)*

1996

NOVEMBER

SAIC acquires Bell Communications Research, Inc. (Bellcore) and changes the name to Telcordia.

1997

JANUARY

SAIC is named the contractor of NASA's Johnson Space Center contract, supporting the manned space program.

1990s

LATE

SAIC develops the Vehicle and Cargo Inspection System (VACIS) technology for the U.S. government. The technology is deployed at seaports and land border points of entry to detect illicit contraband coming into the country.

2000

SAIC sells Network Solutions to VeriSign for $19.6 billion, more than 4,000 times what the firm paid for the company just five years earlier.

In addition to air traffic management, Leidos is also deploying technologies that make air traffic communications more efficient. One of those technologies is Data Comm, a system that is allowing pilots and air traffic controllers to communicate electronically via text. Since the dawn of aviation, air traffic controllers have issued flight instructions to pilots by voice. Pilots then have to repeat those exact instructions back to the controllers in the noisy environment of the cockpit. But if the instructions are repeated back incorrectly, the process has to start all over again. This process can be time-consuming when extrapolated over many flights. With text replacing voice, Data Comm will not only decrease errors due to miscommunication, it will also allow pilots to execute flight instructions faster.

The task of automating the outdated flight progress strip system is another solution Leidos is developing for the FAA. Progress strips are the annotated instructions communicated by the air traffic controllers to the pilots during a shift. Today, these instructions are handwritten on small paper tickets attached to a board, which creates the flight log. The modernization of this process by Leidos will allow the system to go paperless by replacing the manual progress strips with virtual strips that can be moved around using touch screen technology.

"The work that we do is critical, and we have a lot of smart people who work in this business area," said Donna Jones, a systems engineer for air traffic management at Leidos. "Air traffic is safer than ever. Our capability is probably to the six or seven nines. We build our systems to be safety critical and very redundant. We build them to not miss a beat."

Leidos developed the Data Comm system to ensure that pilots and air traffic controllers communicate accurately and efficiently.

2006

The Transportation Safety Administration (TSA) bans liquids, gels, and aerosols in containers larger than 3.4 ounces as part of its 3-1-1 for carry-on procedures. SAIC is contracted to properly handle and dispose of these materials in accordance with Environmental Protection Agency (EPA) regulations.

2015

Leidos gradually replaces the Federal Aviation Administration's (FAA) 40-year-old En Route air traffic control host computer with the state-of-the-art satellite-based En Route Automation Modernization (ERAM) system.

2016

Leidos assumes the Antarctic Support Contract from Lockheed Martin, which provides all of the logistical support for the National Science Foundation (NSF) to the three U.S. research outposts on the continent.

2018

By this year, the company's Reveal Baggage Inspection System is in use by the Transportation Safety Administration (TSA) at more than 200 U.S. airports.

STARS AND STRIPES

SAIC's work with America's Cup winner *Stars and Stripes* was one of the first instances the company gained public recognition for a project, as many of the firm's jobs were classified. Company scientists and engineers worked for three years to design and optimize the yacht's performance, making major breakthroughs along the way in hull and keel design.

The project was spurred after J. Robert Beyster heard the news in 1983 that the United States had lost the America's Cup competition for the first time in its 132-year history. He knew that SAIC's work with the U.S. Navy on hull designs uniquely positioned the firm to contribute to the efforts of U.S. team leader Dennis Conner.

Conner was happy to work with the company to use a computerized model that predicted the yacht's potential wave drag—the first time such a program had been used. When that technology was applied to the yacht's design, success was the result. *Stars and Stripes'* victory in the 1987 America's Cup was a win for the country, Conner's team, and SAIC.

"Our deep involvement with the America's Cup put us in the public eye in a way that we had never before experienced," Beyster later wrote. "It showed others that we were doing good things in our community and that SAIC was a progressive technology company that was on the leading edge of innovation."

Securing Points of Entry

In the Winter of 1988, a devastating act of terrorism occurred that changed the way checked baggage is handled at airports. Pan Am Flight 103 was traveling from Germany to the United States on December 21 when a bomb exploded as the plane flew over Lockerbie, Scotland. All 243 passengers and 16 crew members died, as well as 11 people on the ground.

The United States response to the bombing was swift and firm, and the government asked contractors to submit bids for luggage-inspection devices designed to detect bombs and help prevent similar attacks and loss of life. In 1989, SAIC demonstrated the first luggage-inspection machine to pass FAA-conducted testing. The luggage bomb detection device spotted 95 percent of the simulated explosives attached to luggage in testing.

"The FAA paid $1.1 million for six prototypes, the first of which was installed this month at New York's Kennedy International Airport," the *Washington Post* reported in August 1989. "The others are scheduled for installation by the end of the year at London's Gatwick Airport and air-ports in Frankfurt, West Germany; Detroit; Miami; and San Francisco."

Today, Leidos continues to provide state-of-the-art inspection solutions that not only keep our planes flying safely, but also keep U.S. seaports and borders secure. The company's product portfolio in the Homeland Security and Customs and Border Patrol sectors consists of three main categories: nonintrusive inspection for cargo and passenger vehicles, radiation detection, and computed tomography (CT) explosives detection systems (EDS) for checked and carry-on baggage at airports.

In the nonintrusive inspection category, Leidos has designed and developed the Vehicle and Cargo Inspection System (VACIS) that can scan cargo and passenger vehicles coming into the United States at a rapid rate, whether they come in by land or sea ports of entry. When a vehicle drives through any one of the more than 750 VACIS scanners in the United States, its sensors will accurately detect all illicit contraband, be it drugs, guns, or suspicious amounts of money.

Leidos has more than 1,200 radiation portal monitors deployed in seaports as well as circling the entire northern and southern U.S. borders.

Leidos VACIS technology is used to scan passenger vehicles and cargo, allowing U.S. Customs and Border Patrol operators to identify any and all contraband, including guns and drugs, before it enters the country.

George Walther-Meade, vice president of global sales and marketing for the security and transportation technology group at Leidos, described the high throughput capability and accuracy of the VACIS system at border crossings:

> There are 75 million passenger vehicles coming into the United States on an annual basis. And so what the bad actors do is, they not only attempt to smuggle in contraband and drugs through cargo, they do a lot of that smuggling on a very high volume basis through some of those 75 million passenger vehicles. And so our technology today, and what we're working with the U.S. government on, is instituting a 100 percent scanning of passenger vehicles so you can avoid the historical question when you're crossing the border: "Do you have anything to declare?" Our technology would render that question null and void because we would see firsthand if you're bringing anything into the country and whether or not there's a threat or something that's suspect that needs to be investigated further.

On the radiation detection front, Leidos operates more than 1,200 radiation portal monitors that are installed at the northern and southern borders and at seaports. These portals scan 100 percent of all incoming cargo and passenger vehicles coming into the United States to prevent a dirty bomb from being smuggled into the country. "With radiation detection, what we're looking at is giving our customers the upgraded technology today that will allow them to focus on the threat of special nuclear materials, which is what they are looking for," said Walther-Meade.

Lastly, in the CT EDS category, Leidos is the company credited with developing the luggage x-ray machines that can detect explosives. Currently, the state-of-the-art Leidos Reveal Baggage Inspection System is in use by the Transportation Safety Administration (TSA) at more than 200 U.S. airports.

While there is a zero margin for error in the CT EDS arena, much of the program's success can be attributed to the collaboration between Leidos and the U.S. government to incorporate algorithms into the EDS technology to both combat new threats and to prolong the product's life cycle. "Rather than having to buy a system every seven years, which is originally how the systems and the guidelines were established, it became ten, and then from ten, it became fifteen," said Walther-Meade. "So by us adapting our technology and solutions to the evolving threats, we're able to reduce the cost to the U.S. government of having to recapitalize existing equipment in the field, by extending the life cycle of the system by enhancing the capabilities to detect new and evolving threats."

In terms of the advanced capabilities in inspection solutions, civil business President Angela Heise added:

> Leidos happens to be one of the few companies that has some unique offerings, both from a detection of contraband as well as biometrics capabilities. Because of this, we can provide offerings to our customers that allow them to detect who's coming in and out of the country as well as what they may be bringing, really to help make sure that the citizens of the U.S. and the U.K. are as safe as possible.

Duane Mater, director of client services for the Leidos security and transportation business, with the Reveal CT-120 baggage inspection systems.

While the detection of contraband that could be used to plot an act of terrorism is vital to keeping traveling citizens safe, proper disposal of that contraband is another important function for Leidos. In August 2006, the Department of Homeland Security enacted a ban that would no longer allow passengers to bring liquids, gels, or aerosols in containers larger than 3.4 ounces as part of the TSA's 3-1-1 for carry-on procedures. This created a potentially massive problem for the environment, as each of the confiscated materials or materials that were part of hazardous VAP (Voluntarily Abandoned Property) would need to be properly handled and disposed of in accordance with Environmental Protection Agency (EPA) regulations. "The ban also added a number of new items such as lighters that had to be handled, packaged for transport, and properly disposed of," said James Grant, TSA's hazardous materials program manager. "At the time, SAIC was providing the disposal service for TSA." Though the list of prohibited items has been reduced, the ban and proper disposal of those items by Leidos remains in effect.

The company's distinct skills in creating solutions for civil projects all over the world are not only valued by its customers but are also essential to the safe operation of the world's most important infrastructure systems. The company helps keep the behind-the-scenes transportation operations that many take for granted running smoothly, so travelers don't have to worry about anything but getting where they need to be.

From Energy to the Environment

Energy and environmental issues became important national priorities in the late 1960s and early 1970s. The modern environmental movement shifted concern from preservation to the impact of pollution while an oil embargo spurred new interest in alternative energies such as nuclear power. SAIC would be called upon to employ its expertise in these fields when disaster struck.

On March 28, 1979, Three Mile Island nuclear power plant in Middletown, Pennsylvania, became the site of the worst nuclear disaster in U.S. history when the core of one of the plant's nuclear reactors partially melted. SAIC had extensive knowledge in the field of nuclear energy, from its first military contracts studying radiation effects, to performing detailed risk assessment for the nuclear power industry and regulatory agencies. The company assigned a team of experts to stabilize and monitor the plant.

SAIC's work at Three Mile Island led to additional nuclear-monitoring jobs within the industry and with the Nuclear Regulatory Agency during the 1980s. In 1986, after the Chernobyl disaster, SAIC was called on to assess the safety of U.S. nuclear reactor facilities. The company ultimately became the leading supplier of probabilistic risk assessments for the U.S. nuclear power industry, before branching out to international customers.

The accident at Three Mile Island was not the first time SAIC was called upon during the decade to assist after an environmental accident. In August 1978, New York State officials declared a state of emergency when buried toxins began seeping out of the ground in the Love Canal neighborhood near Niagara Falls. Nearly 1,000 residents left their homes as SAIC assisted in the cleanup of the chemical dumpsite and established the company's expertise in hazardous waste containment.

SAIC would expand into other areas of environmental concern as well. The Department of Labor hired the company to write and conduct studies on occupational health and safety regulations for hazardous chemicals in the workplace. SAIC also worked with the EPA in the area of enforcement as Patrick Bannister, senior vice president, explained:

> It was really SAIC people that had the EPA badges that were doing enforcement. We had the skill sets, the experts. SAIC did extensive work developing water regulations, hazardous waste and water pollution prevention, and recycling in the 1980s, showing once again, when there was a job to be done, SAIC had the skill and qualifications to complete it.

One current project in the energy and environmental sector is its management of the massive 586-square-mile Hanford cleanup site

On March 28, 1979, Three Mile Island's reactor number 2 partially melted. SAIC assigned a team to stabilize and monitor the plant. *(Photo courtesy of CDC/Dr. Ewing.)*

in Washington state. Larger than the city of Los Angeles, the site is home to the production reactors that were used during the Manhattan Project and is where uranium was irradiated and transmuted into plutonium.

The Leidos mission in Hanford is to deliver support to all of the cleanup contractors at the site. "We provide services to everything from their IT to their police force to their fire department," said Heise. "We make sure their roads are clean. We run the utilities for them, and we do all the project management to make sure that they have cranes where they need them. We've been able to save the Department of Energy hundreds of millions of dollars by operating in this common services model across that entire site."

In addition to its work at the Hanford Site, Leidos has also partnered with the Bechtel Corporation in a joint venture in Oakridge, Tennessee (another Manhattan Project site), where it provides engineering services for the Consolidated Nuclear Security organization.

Apart from the on-site projects, Leidos also operates a commercial energy business that provides engineering services to power companies throughout the country. Within this arena, the company has made two significant acquisitions. In 2009, SAIC purchased R. W. Beck Group, a consultancy business that serves the energy, water, wastewater, and solid waste indus-tries. And in 2011, it purchased Patrick Energy Services, a provider of perfor-mance-based transmission and distribution power system solutions to several of the most innovative utility companies in the United States.

In the area of energy efficiency, Leidos administers efficiency programs for several power utilities and efficiency savings programs for a number of major automotive manufacturers. The company is also involved in power restoration. In 2017, Leidos deployed 60 engineers to Florida in the aftermath of Hurricane Irma to help restore power to citizens throughout the state.

A box of transuranic waste is removed from an underground storage trench at the Hanford Site in Washington state, where production reactors were used to irradiate uranium, converting it into plutonium for the Manhattan Project. *(Photo courtesy of U.S. Department of Energy/Flickr.com.)*

SUPPLYING RESOURCES TO THE 7TH CONTINENT

Leidos is one of the only companies in the world that has left its imprint in space and on all seven continents, including Antarctica. The United States has had a presence on the frigid continent since 1956 when the navy traveled there to build outposts for scientific discovery. While scientists from various countries visit the continent each year for the purpose of exploration, no country can lay claim to the land because it is maintained through the Antarctic Treaty.

Today, Leidos operates the world's longest supply chain to support research performed through the National Science Foundation's (NSF) Antarctic Support Contract (ASC). As part of the contract, the company performs all of the logistics planning for the United States at its three research sites on the continent, including one at the South Pole. Each year, Leidos moves 20,000 pounds of cargo, coordinates 2,000 flight missions, and books 3,000 commercial airline tickets to and from the continent.

Whether the company is providing meals or supplying transportation to and from research facilities, research grantees and military personnel rely on Leidos to make sure they have all of the resources they need to accomplish their missions.

Angela Heise, president of the Leidos civil business, described her experience on Antarctica when she visited in 2017:

I had the opportunity to travel to Antarctica during Thanksgiving, and I will tell you, if you ever get down on humanity, going there will absolutely energize you because it's the one place in the world where you see all nations, no matter what their agendas are in the rest of the world, working together to survive and benefit humanity.

Orbiting the Space Program

With the first steps taken on the moon in 1969, the world was spellbound by space travel and the new technology powering flight out of our atmosphere. SAIC scientists were no exception.

In 1972, SAIC got its first taste of the space program when it began working in the space and planetary sciences field in Chicago, Tucson, and Huntsville, Alabama. The company tried to parlay that experience into a larger program in partnership with NASA, bringing on 25-year space agency veteran Neil Hutchinson in 1989 as a corporate vice president. Hutchinson, who had worked as a flight controller for NASA's Apollo missions, helped SAIC forge a contract with the space agency two years later. That NASA partnership continues to this day. The linchpin to scoring the contract originally was Hutchinson's decision to bid for a role with NASA's "Mission to Mars" program, which involved sending unmanned satellites into space to gather data. Hutchinson pored over ways that SAIC could contribute to the project. He later remarked:

> *One thing led to another, and we found an atmospheric sciences support contract at NASA Langley that was coming up to bid. We immersed ourselves*

Leidos delivers approximately 25,000 pounds of payload each year to supply astronauts aboard the International Space Station.

in the competition—really poured our hearts into it—and won the contract
in 1991. It was the largest NASA win in SAIC's history up to that time—
$150 million total, 10 years at $15 million a year. It instantly tripled the size
of the company's assistance to NASA, and it became the foundation that
got the group started.

Today, Leidos provides NASA and the International Space Station (ISS)
with logistical support through its delivery of medical and food services,
research, technology development, engineering, operations, and flight
hardware development to support the health, safety, and productivity of
astronauts. The company also designs, develops, implements, operates,
maintains, and sustains NASA mission control and training systems in
support of human space flight, among its various other functions for the
space agency.

As for the company's next step in space, there is no telling where the
company may see or create new opportunities in the future. Gloria Spikes,
a budget analyst at Leidos who has been involved with NASA projects for
many years, shared her theory:

I see Leidos having a larger role in deep space. I'm sure they are going to be
looking for people out of college who can understand radiation and how it affects
the body. I see the company probably shifting toward the medical aspects of space
since radiation has such a big impact in deep space travel.

Connecting the World

Though Leidos has made a number of successful acquisitions throughout
its history, SAIC's acquisition of Bellcore in November 1996 was particularly
noteworthy. Unlike previous acquisitions, the integration did not instantly
engender a synergy that would bring the two companies together in a
productive way. When SAIC acquired Bellcore, it changed the communications company's name to Telcordia. "While putting a new name on the
company was a relatively easy step, meshing the cultures of Telcordia and
SAIC was not," Beyster later wrote. At issue was Telcordia's culture of
free-spending and providing bonuses to employees simply for their longevity at the company. When contrasted against SAIC's penny-pinching
culture that required employees to meet performance benchmarks to earn
incentives, the two companies were like oil and water.

In 2005, SAIC sold Telcordia. While the divestiture of Telcordia was
unfortunate, the acquisition was largely transformational for the firm as it
greatly expanded the company's profile and offerings in the commercial
telecommunications market. The acquisition also served as a powerful
turning point "because it showed us that SAIC's employee-ownership

culture was not automatically transferable to acquired companies—even if the company was a leading technology company like we were," Beyster later wrote. "Just because the employees bought the stock didn't mean that they bought the idea and culture behind it."

Throughout the years, SAIC continued to advance its civil category by making inroads into untried areas of technology by pinpointing and acquiring companies that would help bolster its expertise in specific markets. Beyster's acquisition model targeted privately held companies that earned under $25 million a year in revenue with two to three owners. The company would average four to five acquisitions a year, but one such acquisition, made in 1995, would propel SAIC to become a major player in the burgeoning Internet space.

Before students earned online degrees, shoppers bought holiday gifts, or customers banked on their smartphones, the U.S. Department of Defense's Advanced Research Projects Agency (ARPA) was developing ARPANET—the precursor to the Internet. Mike Daniels, a former senior vice president and sector vice president for SAIC, who served in the U.S. Navy, was one of the first users of ARPANET in 1969, which he used to send e-mails to university and government contractors during his service. Daniels eventually left the navy, but he kept his eye on ARPANET and watched the technology develop. He recalled those early years:

> *Nobody in the world had any interest, it appeared, in this thing called the Internet, and I went to meetings continually over literally 25 years when ARPA and then the National Science Foundation would have technical meetings about the Internet and how it was being used.*

The Advanced Research Projects Agency Network (ARPANET) was an early packet-switching network and the first network to implement the TCP/IP protocol suite, both of which became the technical foundation of the Internet. Pictured here is an ARPA network map from 1973.

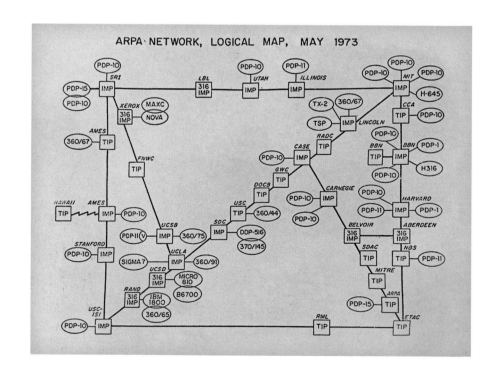

With the acquisition of Network Solutions in 1995, SAIC became a pioneering force in the development of the Internet. Network Solutions was the first—and for a few years, the sole—provider of domain names to the public until the U.S. government declared ownership of the domain name business a monopoly.

Daniels' experience and knowledge paid off for SAIC years later when he joined the company and helped SAIC acquire what would become one of the largest providers of Internet and e-commerce services.

In 1993, the National Science Foundation (NSF) hired the minority-owned small business Network Solutions to develop and run the Internet's domain name registration. Daniels approached Network Solutions and began discussions about a possible acquisition. Two years later, SAIC acquired the company for $4.7 million. The acquisition made SAIC one of the largest providers of Internet and e-commerce services.

After finalizing the acquisition, SAIC worked with the NSF to register domain names with .com, .org, .net, and .edu, which made the company a giant among the burgeoning Internet businesses. However, SAIC's interest wasn't focused on Network Solutions' Internet naming unit. Instead, the company believed that Network Solutions' experience building data networks would be an excellent complement to SAIC's competencies. "With $25 million in annual telecommunications consulting revenues, 400 employees located within a stone's throw of SAIC's Northern Virginia offices, and name-brand clients such as NationsBank and AT&T, purchasing Network Solutions made sense for many different reasons," Beyster later wrote.

In the Internet's early days, the NSF had subsidized the cost of registering domain names, which meant customers were able to reserve these names for free. Fortuitously, the very same year that SAIC acquired Network Solutions, the NSF began allowing Network Solutions to charge

A domain name registry is a database of all domain names and the associated registrant information in the top-level domains of the Internet. Instrumental in SAIC purchasing domain registrar Network Solutions in 1995, Mike Daniels recognized this database as being the "keys to the kingdom."

customers a $50 fee to register a domain name for one year, or $100 for a two-year reservation. The agreement coincided with a burst in the Internet's popularity as companies realized the value of an online presence. Internet registrations skyrocketed. Within four years, registrations soared nearly six million times, making the Network Solutions acquisition a quickly growing cash cow and, by virtue of the acquisition, adding significantly to SAIC's coffers.

Daniels believed that domain names were the core functionality of the Internet and that they would be valuable at some point because the Internet could not work without the WHOIS database, which was part of NSF's contract with Network Solutions. The WHOIS database is the core function of the Internet, matching a domain name such as Google.com to the underlying IP address. "Without the database, no one can access the Internet. These are the keys to the kingdom," said Daniels.

At the dot-com boom's pinnacle in the year 2000, SAIC sold its remaining portion of Network Solutions to VeriSign for $2.6 billion. Regarding the world's first domain registrar's purchase and sale, Beyster wrote:

This experience reinforced our core value of allowing and encouraging individual entrepreneurs to find and act on opportunities—wherever they might occur.

Combating Cyber Crime

Though Leidos is one of the companies recognized for bringing the Internet to the masses, today's Internet has become a gateway into our businesses and our homes, and sometimes that gateway lets in more than we bargain for. Hacks on major companies have exposed billions of user accounts and cyber crime damages are expected to cost businesses $2 trillion annually by the year 2019. Ever since an online presence became a must for businesses, Leidos has been at the forefront of efforts to protect companies from cyber crime.

In 1996, the company joined forces with 146-year-old security company Pinkerton, Inc., to protect clients from internal and external threats. Clients had 24-hour access to a collection of security services constructed to identify and assess security risks, design security solutions and counter-measures, and implement security measures with access controls, firewalls, and encryption. The SAIC–Pinkerton security service enabled businesses to compete in the international marketplace while keeping their assets safe.

Beyster remarked on the service's capabilities:

Our expertise is available around the clock to assist clients in preventing network, information systems, and Internet attacks from computer hackers, criminals, and insiders, as well as to provide real-time, command-center services when attacks do occur.

In 1996, SAIC joined forces with Pinkerton, Inc., to protect clients from internal and external cyber threats, providing services designed to identify, assess, and address security risks.

Today, Leidos develops platforms for threat intelligence management, insider threat detection, industrial control systems management, and advanced threat monitoring.

Solutions for a Complicated World

As the world becomes increasingly complex, Leidos is continually developing solutions to meet the critical challenges of today and tomorrow.

As new modes of transportation are imagined and new threats against national security surface, whether online or off-line, Leidos will continue to offer and develop innovative IT, security, and threat mitigation solutions to companies and government organizations that need them, just as Beyster envisioned when he founded the company. "Meeting the customer's mission, coming up with solutions, or solving problems that nobody thinks are solvable are characteristics that Dr. Beyster certainly invoked in our culture, and that still exists today," said Jim Moos, deputy president for the civil business.

In terms of customer service, Brian Anderson, the NAS Integration Support Contract (NISC) program manager for the FAA, said of his working relationship with Leidos:

> *Leidos is one of the largest service providers for the federal government, and the company drives improvement via strong relationships with its customers, as evidenced by the NISC Contract Management Office. Despite being a large business, I believe they treat each customer as if they are the only customer, with care and commitment as if they were still a small business.*

From a business perspective, Beyster's concept of applying science to solutions with an emphasis on innovative selling and excellence in customer service is a goal Leidos has realized. From a humanity perspective, the critical solutions developed by Leidos in civil markets can be credited with improving and safeguarding the lives of every citizen of the world, whether they know it or not. ■

CHAPTER FOUR

HEALTHCARE

Using data analytics, our team came up with a hypothesized cure for a type of neuroblastoma, and ultimately, that cure was developed into a therapy, and it was effective. So in many ways, our team has figured out at least one type of cancer through their wonderful work.

Jonathan Scholl
PRESIDENT OF THE LEIDOS HEALTH BUSINESS

WHEN SAIC WAS ESTABLISHED IN 1969, THE COM-pany created a subsidiary known as JRB Associates to offer lower bidding rates for its non-defense projects. Among the earliest jobs JRB Associates landed were contracts with two National Institutes of Health (NIH) branches: the National Cancer Institute (NCI) and the National Heart, Lung, and Blood Institute (NHLBI). These contracts launched the early work that would become the company's esteemed healthcare business.

Not long thereafter, the company brought in a contract studying radiation-based cancer therapy for the Los Alamos National Laboratory, which demonstrated J. Robert Beyster's ability to marry his interest in nuclear energy and physics with his growing interest in the healthcare arena. The studies led to a successful consultation business for medical cancer radiation protocols using electronic linear accelerators and proton accelerators for cancer therapy. Several hospitals, such as MD Anderson Cancer Center in Houston, commissioned SAIC to help design their radiation-shielded facilities and write their linear accelerator specifications. SAIC's business grew rapidly with little advanced planning.

Today, as Leidos, the company's work in healthcare has expanded dramatically and the firm is now the ninth largest healthcare IT provider

Opposite: Then-SAIC and Leidos staff include doctorate-level scientific and analytical professionals who perform cutting-edge research to cure diseases, develop vaccines, and test medications via clinical trials. *(Photo by Olivier Le Queinec, Shutterstock.)*

Jonathan Scholl serves as president of the health business at Leidos.

in the United States. Leidos handles the IT strategy and advisory services for hospitals all over the world, keeps patient information safe via electronic health records and cybersecurity support, and keeps its clients on track with regulatory requirements. In health information technology alone, Leidos has thousands of employees in hospitals around the country, training staff on how to implement and use electronic health records systems. The company's workforce also includes doctorate-level scientific and analytical professionals who perform groundbreaking research to cure diseases, develop vaccines, and test medications via clinical trials. No matter what aspect of healthcare is taking place, Leidos has probably contributed to it in some way, shape, or form.

In addition to providing essential healthcare services and solutions, Jonathan Scholl, president of the Leidos health business, sees the company's depth and breadth of work as a benefit to customers:

> *I believe one of our great opportunities in the Health group is that we can take the phenomenal work that we do in the commercial sector and pull it into the federal work we do, and take the outstanding work we do in the federal sector and pull it into our commercial work.*

Healthcare Roots

When SAIC first formed its JRB Associates subsidiary in 1969, it was unclear where the new unit would take the company, but it quickly became apparent that the firm's knowledge was needed in the healthcare field. The MD Anderson Radiation Center became one of the five largest radiation facilities and hospitals in the United States, and SAIC's work for the hospital

1969

SAIC creates a subsidiary known as JRB Associates, which lowers bidding rates for the company's non-defense projects. Among JRB's first contracts were jobs with the National Cancer Institute (NCI) and the National Heart, Lung, and Blood Institute, creating the early building blocks of the Leidos healthcare business.

1970s

SAIC assists several hospitals, such as MD Anderson Cancer Center in Houston, Texas, in designing their radiation-shielded facilities.

1970

Leidos wins a contract studying radiation-based cancer therapy for the Los Alamos National Laboratory.

1972

U.S. President Richard Nixon declares war on cancer and increases the National Cancer Institute's budget from $200 million to $1 billion a year.

The company's employees provide services and solutions in health information technology, population health risk management and case management, health analytics, life sciences, and public health.

provided the company key credibility for bidding on new contracts. "In 1972, when Nixon came in, he declared the war on cancer, and he took the cancer budget from $200 million to a billion in one year, and so there was a big ramp-up going on, and they were doing all the planning associated with that and setting up the cancer centers," recalled SAIC executive Jim Russell, who joined the company that same year. Russell was instrumental in helping SAIC diversify the firm's services into areas such as transportation, law enforcement, and healthcare. He visited colleges, pharmacies, and other places that had individual healthcare systems to evaluate and learn from their processes. It was an exciting time for those involved.

Patrick Bannister had just joined SAIC as a member of JRB Associates when he began working on a strategic plan for the NCI. "It was very interesting to be in on the ground floor to put together the strategy, the plan.

1988

CREDIT: OFFICIAL MARINE CORPS PHOTO BY CPL. JUSTIN M. MARTINEZ.*

SAIC wins its first billion-dollar contract to create the Department of Defense's (DoD) Composite Health Care System deployed to more than 500 DoD medical facilities worldwide.

1995

Kaiser Permanente selects SAIC to design its strategic healthcare IT platform, driven by SAIC's healthcare IT system success.

1995

SAIC wins a contract with the National Cancer Institute's largest research center, allowing 1,300 SAIC experts to work every day on cancer and AIDS research.

1997

CREDIT: PHOTO BY VIRIN: 287513-J-WRI05-562.JPG.*

AUGUST

SAIC wins a DoD (Health Affairs) contract worth about $200 million to support its hardware and software applications.

*The appearance of U.S. Department of Defense (DoD) visual information does not imply or constitute DoD endorsement.

How was NCI going to work? What was it going to be? What type of areas were we going to be looking at?" recalled Bannister. At the time experts were not sure what caused cancer—a virus, environmental exposure, genetics. But whether it was the National Cancer Institute, the Environmental Protection Agency (EPA), or the Occupational Safety and Health Administration (OSHA), SAIC was usually there at the onset helping to build, organize, and set in motion new initiatives.

SAIC won multiple contracts with health-focused government agencies in the 1970s and 1980s, including the U.S. Department of Health, Education, and Welfare (HEW), the precursor to today's Department of Health and Human Services.

The key to SAIC's success in the healthcare field was in strategically building the right workforce. Russell focused on hiring individuals who were medical, in addition to those who were computer experts, as he explained:

Back at that time, in the early seventies, database management systems were just starting, and I evaluated and saw they were going to go into all of the government organizations in Washington, D.C., and elsewhere, so I hired specialists with database-management backgrounds.

He also set up SAIC's first system center to give employees hands-on experience before tackling the actual job, which was vital to growing the business. Once SAIC proved its expertise in the cancer arena, the company

was able to win another six contracts with additional health-focused government agencies, including the U.S. Department of Health, Education, and Welfare (HEW), which was the precursor to today's Department of Health and Human Services. SAIC provided information management for several agencies within HEW, helped build the National Blood Bank System, and worked within the National Health Statistical System.

1999

SAIC acquires Oacis Healthcare, which makes software for electronic medical records.

1999

NOVEMBER

SAIC launches Health eTrust alliance to help the healthcare industry comply with the HIPAA requirements.

2008

SAIC secures the largest single research contract the Department of Health and Human Services has ever awarded. The contract—for up to $5.2 billion—tasks SAIC with helping operate and provide technical support to the NCI's research and development center.

2012

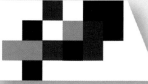

SAIC acquires maxIT Healthcare, North America's largest independent consulting firm specializing in healthcare IT, for $473 million.

Pioneering Health IT

Back in 1995, most people had never heard of healthcare IT, electronic health records, or e-prescribing, but as doctors were scribbling notes about their patients on paper charts, SAIC was at the forefront of establishing the country's burgeoning electronic records system. That was the year Kaiser Permanente selected the company to design its strategic healthcare IT platform, driven by how well SAIC's healthcare IT system had performed for the Department of Defense (DoD). Although Kaiser was interested in gaining digital access to its medical records, the healthcare company was also seeking to partner with a firm that understood its business processes. Enter SAIC.

SAIC was at the forefront of establishing the country's burgeoning electronic records system. In 1995 the firm was selected to design Kaiser Permanente's strategic health care IT platform.

2014

The Food and Drug Administration's (FDA) Office of Regulatory Affairs (ORA) awards Leidos with the project to modernize the Agency's legacy applications for its Mission Accomplishment and Regulatory Compliance Service (MARCS) program.

2015

Leidos wins a $4.3 billion contract from the DoD to deliver its Electronic Health Records (EHR) system.

2016

careC2 pathways

Development begins on the Leidos careC2 program, a groundbreaking enterprise platform that will help healthcare systems integrate all of their data into one application.

2017

APRIL

Leidos wins a $29 million contract with the Department of Veterans Affairs (VA), supporting the agency's IT infrastructure.

Thanks to the company's history in the healthcare field, SAIC employees understood how hospital departments were able to work together, and were able to help Kaiser staff members transition to a distributed computing infrastructure from the existing system, which had been built around mainframe computers. The company's work with Kaiser Permanente helped SAIC establish itself in the private healthcare industry after working with government healthcare entities for so many years, opening up a new line of business for the company.

After its successful work with Kaiser Permanente, SAIC earned contracts with Saint Luke's Hospital in Kansas City, where the facility worked to merge its hospital and outpatient locations. Additionally, SAIC designed a system in Saskatchewan, Canada, that allowed all healthcare providers in the province access to electronic medical records. "SAIC was no longer the dark horse in every contract competition," the company later wrote.

Supporting Military Health

Today, Leidos is the largest third-party integrator of Electronic Health Records (EHR) in the United States. In addition to the company's work on medical records systems in the commercial sector, Leidos has a proud history of supporting the health record system for the DoD that includes the company's first billion-dollar contract in 1988. Jim Russell recalled SAIC's attempt to manage the DoD's Composite Health Care System (CHCS):

> *I had quite a few people working with me then in the health area who advised me not to do it. They said it would ruin my career. But I said, "I'm going for it. You've got to stick your neck out a little bit."*

After working for 18 months on a proposal that measured 65 inches high when printed out, SAIC won the monumental job. The company would go on to maintain and sustain the CHCS and Alpha platform for 30 years before it would need to be reimagined for the digital era.

In 2015, the company won the $4.3 billion contract from the DoD to implement the Defense Health Management System Modernization. "It was time to modernize it and we're pleased and proud to be part of that program," Scholl said.

Cerner Corporation and Accenture Federal joined a Leidos staff of 7,000, which included healthcare consultants, biostatisticians, data analytics, and IT experts. The adept team created Military Health System (MHS) GENESIS, a single health record for service members, veterans, and their families, which connects medical and dental information through the sequence of care, from injury through treatment at a military facility. MHS GENESIS also provides a

patient portal, a secure website for patients to access health information, including managing appointments and exchanging messages with doctors. The MHS GENESIS Patient Portal launched at Fairchild Air Force Base in February 2017 and has been deployed at other initial fielding sites throughout the Pacific Northwest, including Naval Health Clinic Oak Harbor, Naval Hospital Bremerton, and Madigan Army Medical Center.

Regarding the company's view of the future and its position as a science and technology leader in the healthcare market, Scholl told *Healthcare Informatics* at the time:

The company has a long history of supporting the Department of Veterans Affairs, the largest integrated healthcare system in the United States. *(Photo by Monkey Business Images/Shutterstock.)*

> *We have a very deliberate viewpoint of what the next generation of healthcare is going to look like, as a group, and we're going to grow because we have a strategy. And we're investing in leadership to grow it. We solve important national problems in several markets, including the healthcare market, and at our core, we are not a platform company, but rather a science and technology company. And in health, we want to solve the hardest problems in health as they relate to analytics, to human factors, and we're aiming to do that.*

Streamlining FDA Inspections

In addition to monitoring food and drug products developed within the United States, the Food and Drug Administration (FDA) has multiple initiatives for monitoring products that are imported into the country. The scope of these FDA initiatives includes protecting consumers from unsafe foods through research and methods development, inspection, voluntary destruction, sampling, recall, seizure, injunction, and criminal prosecution.

To streamline the outcomes of these initiatives, in 2014 the FDA's Office of Regulatory Affairs (ORA) tasked Leidos with modernizing the federal agency's more than 30 legacy applications for its Mission Accomplishment and Regulatory Compliance Services (MARCS) program. In support of the FDA's centers for drug evaluation and research, biologics, medical devices, tobacco products, and veterinary medicine work, Leidos has developed a full suite of software applications to ensure regulated entities are in compliance, and imports coming into the United States are properly inspected. The information the software gathers is shared between the FDA's ORA and Customs and Border Protection (CBP).

Edouard Benjamin, vice president of program management in the Leidos health business, explained the import process and the role that Leidos software plays in the MARCS program:

> When companies are importing, let's say food, they have to register that product and the supply chain information. Then they alert the FDA and the CBP when those shipments are coming in. Those agencies then have to make the decisions about which shipments are going to be visually inspected and which ones can be fast-tracked. The software that we build not only supports the inspectors on the ground to determine that, it also supports the regulators within the FDA that task the inspectors, as well as the regulators within the divisions that manage the coordination of imports versus domestic activity within the country.

Walter Harris, the former deputy commissioner for operations and chief operating officer of the FDA said of the company's work on the MARCS program:

> When I came to the FDA in 2012, the MARCS program was hemorrhaging from a lot of losses. The system was not working well. The procedures and staff were not working well. ... We put a new requirement out on the street, competed it out, and Leidos won the bid. And since they came on board, the MARCS system has grown by leaps and bounds. They really proved that a company like Leidos that had the deep background can come in and understand the needs of our customer, and could create systems and tools that could be used by our employees to help interact properly with our industry partners. They did a pretty good job of turning that around.

Leidos works closely with the Food and Drug Administration on critical initiatives inspecting imported products, including popular fruits such as avocados.

The careC2 Pathways workflow follows the patient through their course of care, monitors the patient's status and progress through each phase of the medical care treatment and/or procedure, and ultimately measures how well the care-providers are performing.

Connecting
All Points of Care

One of the toughest challenges Leidos is working to solve is one no other company has dared to take on—digitizing the full suite of healthcare management services to optimize longitudinal patient care. In 2016, Leidos began development of its groundbreaking enterprise platform, known as careC2. The platform will enable health systems to better integrate data, ingest information from disparate sources, normalize it, and then use a business logic layer with a user interface design that can be changed on the fly to meet the specific needs of customers.

CareC2, in which the C2 stands for Command and Control based on a platform algorithm that originated with the company's defense business, will ensure that patients are being provided with the best and most efficient acute, ambulatory, or home care possible. At a granular level, careC2's central application, known as Pathways, consumes big data that is collected from a myriad of sources within a healthcare system. The application then shares that data with healthcare administrators, nurses, and doctors in the effort to save patients—and the health systems that are serving them—time and money through the delivery of proven data-driven care.

HEALTHCARE ACQUISITIONS

Leidos has built its healthcare business both organically and through acquisitions, many of which have helped the firm move into new specialty areas. For instance, in 1999, SAIC acquired Oacis Healthcare, which makes software for electronic medical records, and, in 2012, the firm acquired maxIT Healthcare for $473 million. At the time, maxIT was the largest independent consulting company specializing in healthcare IT in North America.

"We've always prided ourselves on taking on problems of national significance and finding solutions; healthcare is no different," said Steve Comber, general manager of SAIC's health solutions business at the time.

Fay Hung, Leidos director of product management for the careC2 program, provided some practical insights into the real-world application of the Pathways platform:

> With our analytics, we're able to provide health systems with data that says, "Last week you had 30 joint replacements. This is how you were able to improve length of stay by three hours, and here are the outlier cases." Maybe it's because these patients had complications. Or maybe the nurse forgot to ambulate a patient, which is why that patient ended up adding another 15 hours to their length of stay.

Hung also spoke about the application of the Pathways technology in the area of monitoring the logistics of medical equipment:

> When you go to an emergency room, you're often waiting around for a long time. It's not because the doctors aren't available. It's because the radiology, EKG, or the ultrasound machines aren't available. But a hospital might have three more in another wing that aren't being utilized. To mitigate this, we can track the availability of equipment to improve patient throughput.

In addition to the Pathways application, the careC2 program is also developing another groundbreaking data-driven application under its umbrella. Named Quantum, the application is a personnel forecasting platform that will allow health systems to save money on last-minute staffing changes, which can become very expensive. Quantum essentially serves as a preventive staffing tool to ensure that a hospital has enough full-time employees and enough floaters scheduled to cover certain shifts. Using Quantum, staffing trends are predicted three to nine months out using historical operational data to determine staffing needs in the future.

As innovation in the health sector continues to grow exponentially, the careC2 platform, through the use of its Pathways and Quantum applications, is aiming to lead the way in the healthcare management solutions arena. "We're a startup within a $10 billion company," said Hung. "If we had gone out into the market and asked for funding for projects like these, I'm not sure anybody would have invested in us, but our company took a chance because we think big, and we're gaining traction."

Working to Find a Cure

In addition to its work on the technology side of the healthcare sector, Leidos is also heavily invested in medical sciences. For more than two decades, Leidos has been working with the National Cancer Institute (NCI) operating its largest research center—the Frederick National Laboratory for Cancer Research. The company's responsibilities at the laboratory have ranged from security, to agenda setting, to research.

In 1995, the company signed a contract with the NCI's largest research center, committing 1,300 SAIC experts to work every day on cancer and AIDS research. SAIC attributed the contract win to its experienced management-level staff, led by Peter Fischinger, who was the former deputy director of the NCI. "We were able to bring an extremely qualified management team to the table," SAIC spokeswoman Sue Volek told *The Washington Post* at the time. "We play by the rules, we went through the competitive process like any-one else, and we feel we won because we offered the best value to the government."

In 2008, a new contract with NCI led SAIC to a record-sized partnership. The company won what was said to be the largest single research contract that the Department of Health and Human Services had ever awarded. The contract was worth up to $5.2 billion over the course of 10 years to help operate and provide technical support to the NCI's Frederick National Laboratory for Cancer Research in Frederick, Maryland. "At the Frederick facility, we're work-ing to develop a portfolio of biologics, generally speaking, peptides, which are small proteins that address the cancer and infectious disease market,"

SAIC has worked at the Frederick National Laboratory for Cancer for more than two decades to find a cure for the disease.

said Doug Barton, senior vice president, chief technology officer, and chief engineer within the Leidos health business. "We've got patented molecules now and we're working to establish sort of a bio-tech business model where we can monetize those molecules in ways that are beneficial to the company, but also, frankly, some of them have great promise to address some real public health issues like cancer."

Retired Major General Arnold Punaro, former SAIC executive vice president and general manager for Washington operations, said of the company's mission-focused work in cancer research:

The people who work at Leidos and its predecessor organizations are focused on the mission first because the vast majority of our work is for the U.S. government, whether it's on the national security side or the civil side.

THE FREDERICK NATIONAL LABORATORY FOR CANCER RESEARCH

Leidos Biomedical Research operates the Frederick National Laboratory for Cancer Research—a federal laboratory sponsored by the National Cancer Institute (NCI). The facility focuses on researching cancer with the goal of innovating and finding solutions to improve the health of patients who are suffering from the deadly disease.

SAIC forged the contract with the NCI over 20 years ago, committing 1,300 company experts to work every day on cancer research. The team has consistently performed high-level studies on the various forms of the disease, placing the facility on the leading edge of discovering a means of prevention or potential cures.

For example, a lot of people don't realize this, but Leidos runs the most important cancer research society in the world, the National Cancer Institute, and we have over 12,000 of the top doctors and scientists in the world working to cure this dreaded disease. So every day, the Leidos employees come to work basically to try to make the world a better place and to accomplish the missions of our government.

SAIC has provided valuable research for both the National Cancer Institute and the National Heart, Lung, and Blood Institute.

As part of the NCI contract, SAIC–Frederick provided operations and technical support in three essential areas, which were translational research and development, basic research, and preclinical research and development. At the time, SAIC–Frederick was providing support to over 300 clinical trials and operating a pilot program in 14 states, studying how community hospitals could bring the most recent, fact-based cancer care to inner-city, rural, and underserved patients. The new contract would build upon the hard work that SAIC had already performed for NCI over the years.

"We appreciate the confidence NCI has shown in SAIC over the past 13 years and look forward to continuing our work to help deliver preventive, diagnostic, and therapeutic products to cancer patients," said Charles Koontz, SAIC group president, at the time.

Currently, much of the company's work in the cancer arena is focused on RAS, a gene that is mutated in about 30 percent of human cancers. The company's research of the RAS gene, as well as the development of new cancer-detecting technologies, has reinvigorated efforts by biotech companies and the pharmaceutical industry to identify inhibitors that will be active against tumors with the mutant gene. "The interest in RAS as a target for developing better treatment for cancer really has been brought to the forefront by the RAS initiative at Leidos," said Dr. Doug Lowy, former acting director of the NCI. "Although we have known about mutant RAS for a long time, we have not been successful at developing inhibitors against it. So many people who die from cancer are dying, at least in part, because their tumors have mutant RAS. If we could target it, we would be very far ahead in cancer treatment."

Today, Leidos continues to provide scientific and technological innovations, resources, and staff who work tirelessly toward cures or methods of prevention for the various forms of cancer, as Dr. Lowy described:

> *There are more than one and a half million people in the United States who develop cancer each year and about 600,000 people who die from cancer each year. Of course, that's too many people who die, but more than 60 percent of people who develop cancer are cured from their disease. Our goals are to try to prevent the cancer from developing, and then when cancer does develop, to be able to successfully treat many more people, and in addition, to decrease the side effects from the treatment. That's what our goals are. And Leidos plays a key role in those areas.*

Enhancing Veteran Care

Although the Leidos healthcare business often flies under the radar among members of the public, the division is making excellent progress toward helping cure diseases and enabling healthcare systems such as those of the Department of Defense and the Department of Veterans Affairs to run more efficiently. "They call 1-800-Tricare. They probably think they're talking to a military nurse, but they're talking to Leidos," explained Patrick Bannister.

In 2016, the Leidos healthcare business logged $1.7 billion in revenue, with 69 percent coming from government contracts and 31 percent from commercial. And in April 2017, Leidos won a $29 million contract with the Department of Veterans Affairs (VA), supporting the IT infrastructure of the agency. The VA is the largest integrated healthcare system in the United States, with more than 1,200 healthcare facilities, including 170 VA medical centers and over a thousand outpatient clinics, serving at least 9 million enrolled veterans every year. "This program is vitally important to enabling

The Department of Veterans Affairs healthcare system, supported by Leidos, serves more than 9 million veterans each year.

the VA to provide the best care to our nation's veterans, and we're proud to support our customer's most important mission," Scholl said.

The company is likely to expand its VA wins beyond electronic healthcare and into the clinical realm as well. "A notable program win in the quarter that was possible through success in our efforts includes a re-compete contract with the Veterans Benefits Administration supported by our Health group," said Leidos CEO Roger Krone during the company's second-quarter conference call in 2017. "This contract allows us to continue our decades-long commitment to serving the nation's veterans with critical clinical support."

That support includes a program that performs medical examinations to help qualify veterans for benefits. "Are they 20 percent disabled or 100 percent disabled given their service-related experience injuries? We do those examinations and have been doing it for 15 years, and it's just another phenomenal opportunity," explained Scholl. The program continues to grow under dedicated leadership to ensure veterans receive the care promised to them.

A Complex Mission

Leidos jumped into the healthcare industry early in the company's history, as Beyster looked to incorporate his experience in nuclear science with medicine.

The company would secure contracts with multiple governmental agencies as well as private entities, but their mission was the same no matter the client. Whether it was an active duty military person, their family members, a veteran, or a civilian, the company's goal was to transform the healthcare industry while providing the best service and treatment possible.

"We are a science, technology, engineering, and mission company," said Barton. "When I say we support the mission, I mean we have people sitting in operations centers sitting side by side with our customers performing that mission. I think you can find companies that focus on mission and companies that focus on engineering, but you would be hard-pressed to find a company that spans the science, technology, engineering, and mission components of our customer base all in one company.

The mission is complex, demanding the knowledge and skills of the best and brightest, and Leidos is constantly looking for new talent to add to its workforce. "I think we're probably the largest recruiter of college grads out of Central Florida, where they have a phenomenal engineering program around electrical grid design and engineering," said Scholl. Basic research in

SAIC was responsible for supporting hospitals across the country as well as government agencies in transitioning the health record system from paper to electronic.

science around sensors and phenomenology, data analytics, hard-core systems engineering, and systems design demands the very best, and the very best is who Leidos is looking for.

In terms of the company's future in the healthcare field, Scholl added:

> *I think in 10 years what you'll see out of Leidos Health is a meaningful impact known by all of its customers worldwide as a thought leader and service provider in the transformation of healthcare.*

Leidos has decades of experience putting emphasis on healthcare and acting on opportunities. As the country increasingly moves toward a more complex and intricate healthcare system, Leidos will be there to ensure that patients, physicians, insurers, and everyone else can move smoothly through the landscape. Whether it's integrating IT services, providing clinical assistance, or finding cures for the world's most devastating diseases, the individuals at Leidos will continue to discover and provide innovative well-being solutions. ∎

CHAPTER FIVE

DEFENSE & INTELLIGENCE

In previous generations, in national security, most investments were in exquisite solutions that took years to develop and cost billions of dollars. These solutions would be focused against one adversary. More recently, with everything being about data, information technology, and software development, the emphasis is on providing solutions quicker and at a more affordable price by developing them in a modular way so they can be targeted against any adversary.

Timothy Reardon
FORMER PRESIDENT OF THE LEIDOS DEFENSE & INTELLIGENCE BUSINESS

D
EFENSE HAS BEEN PART OF THE LEIDOS DNA SINCE ITS early days, when one of the company's first contracts was a $70,000 project with the Defense Atomic Support Agency (DASA), which handled nuclear energy. In just a little more than a decade, the company became one of the country's fastest growing and most successful defense firms. Leidos is still involved in these endeavors and continues to stay on the forefront of keeping the United States safe in a variety of ways.

From helping the government create night-vision goggles and anti-missile systems, to keeping New York City safe after the terrorist attacks on September 11, 2001, Leidos has solved problems and launched innovations that help protect Americans and the world at large. Even those who have not heard of Leidos have benefited from their technologies, just by driving on the roads or visiting airports, knowing that the U.S. military, government agencies, and private firms have the tools they need to win every battle.

Retired U.S. Air Force Major General and later-SAIC Executive Vice President Robert "Rosie" Rosenberg reiterated:

Having served inside the government for 30 years and subsequently chairing and sitting on numerous advisory boards, I've seen how critical it is to attract, retain, and grow systems engineers and those with systems integra-

Opposite: Mine Resistant Ambush Protected (MRAP) vehicles being outfitted at the firm's facility in Charleston, South Carolina. Designed to protect the occupants from ambush-style attacks, MRAP vehicles support urban combat operations and multi-mission operations in Afghanistan and Iraq.

Timothy Reardon served as president of the Defense & Intelligence Group from 2016–2018.

tion expertise. Companies like Leidos have an opportunity to make a significant impact doing important work—helping land, naval, and air combat warriors keep us free.

Advancing Precision

Two advancements that have been crucial to national security are precision navigation and speed. Retired Major General Arnold Punaro, former SAIC executive vice president and general manager for Washington operations, fought as a young second lieutenant in the U.S. Marine Corps during the Vietnam War. "We didn't have the electronic precision navigation that they have today, a lot of which depends on companies like Leidos. And then the second thing would be speed, the speed at which you can process data, the speed at which you can compute solutions, the speed at which you can bring a kinetic weapon to bear."

One of the company's earliest major software development jobs was for the United States Army Missile Command in the 1970s. Before the decade closed out, a team of more than 1,200 SAIC employees provided technical support and management assistance to the Department of Defense's (DoD) Joint Missile Program to develop the cruise missile.

Paul Coakley, who was assigned to the Joint Cruise Missile Program Office (JCMPO) in December 1983, was the primary within the Cruise Missile Office for national, theater and tactical intelligence agencies, commands, and program offices related to imagery tasking, collection, and dissemination. "The performance of my duties would not have been possible without the expertise and knowledge of the many SAIC support teams," said Coakley. "Leidos has supported the Cruise Missile Program

1970s

SAIC wins one of its earliest major software development jobs for the U.S. Army Missile Command, which would later become the Tomahawk Cruise Missile Program (CMP).

1983

President Ronald Reagan announces the Strategic Defense Initiative (SDI), a missile-defense program that will serve to protect the country from a Soviet nuclear attack.

1985

The Pentagon asks SAIC to research how the SDI's anti-missile system should be designed. As part of the $5 million contract, SAIC's experts immerse themselves in the program, which the media refers to as "Star Wars."

1990s

SAI Technology creates the Lightweight Computer Unit (LCU), a laptop customized for the Army that is rugged enough to make its way through rough terrain.

(CMP) since its inception in the mid- to late 1970s, always with great accolades from senior leadership within CMP."

Punaro said of the company's contribution to the development of the CMP:

> *They're the ones who designed the brains of the Tomahawk Cruise Missile that allows it to turn corners and fly in with precision at subsonic speeds. They've had roles in some of the most important military operations our nation has been involved in. ... If you want to work on something that's cutting edge, something that's going to make the United States safer, you want to work at Leidos because that's the kind of work they do every day.*

SAIC developed precision navigation systems for cruise missiles, enabling them to turn corners and fly to their targets at subsonic speeds. *(U.S. Navy photo by Photographers Mate 2nd Class Daniel J. McLain (RELEASED).)**

1994

SAIC acquires the government unit of Ideas, Inc., which provides complex telecommunications products and services to the Department of Defense.

1994

APRIL

SAIC is awarded the Outstanding Prime Contractor Award from the Defense Contractor Management Area Office of the Defense Logistics Agency for achievements in SAIC's Small Business Program.

2001

SEPTEMBER 11

Four coordinated terrorist attacks claim the lives of nearly 3,000 victims in New York, Pennsylvania, and the Pentagon in Washington, D.C.

2001

CREDIT: U.S. NAVY PHOTO BY PHOTOGRAPHER'S MATE 1ST CLASS GREG MESSIER (RELEASED).*

OCTOBER 7

In response to the September 11 terrorist attacks, the U.S. launches Operation Enduring Freedom, beginning the war on terror in Afghanistan.

On March 23, 1983, President Ronald Reagan publicly announced the Strategic Defense Initiative, an advanced missile-defense system to protect the United States from a Soviet nuclear attack. *(Photo Courtesy of U.S. National Archives and Records Administration, ARC Identifier: 198536.)*

"Star Wars"

In addition to SAIC's involvement in the Tomahawk Cruise Missile Program, one of the company's most high-profile projects arrived in the 1980s with the massive Strategic Defense Initiative (SDI) program. In 1983, President Ronald Reagan announced plans for a missile-defense system to protect the country from a Soviet nuclear attack. SAIC was one of the more highly regarded companies at the time, taking on many jobs related to the military that included analyzing how different parts of a weapons system fit together, writing computer software, and handling complex purchases. The Pentagon asked the company in 1985 to research how the SDI (dubbed "Star Wars" by the media) anti-missile system should be designed. As part of the $5 million contract, SAIC's experts immersed themselves in the program.

The project involved determining how the government could develop lasers and other weapons that could deploy from space to destroy Soviet missiles if they were poised to attack the United States. Fortunately, the country didn't end up needing to call on the Star Wars defense system, but the United States was much safer thanks to SAIC's research.

Post-Cold War Growth

Much of the company's strength lies in its diverse talent pool, which has in many ways allowed the company to exponentially grow its business and adapt to the needs and demands of its customers quickly and competently. When the Soviet Union collapsed in December 1991, the company shifted its priorities. No longer was SAIC helping defend the country from a nuclear superpower; now the company was tasked with analyzing and

2003

CREDIT: U.S. NAVY PHOTO BY PHOTOGRAPHER'S MATE 1ST CLASS MICHAEL W. PENDERGRASS. (RELEASED)*

MARCH 20

The United States launches Operation Iraqi Freedom, eventually overthrowing the government of Saddam Hussein.

2007

The Department of Defense begins the Mine-Resistant Ambush Protected (MRAP) program, created in response to attacks from improvised explosive devices during the Iraq and Afghanistan wars.

2008

APRIL

SAIC is awarded a Defense Intelligence Agency contract worth up to $1 billion to develop technology for analyzing military intelligence.

2008

CREDIT: U.S. ARMY PHOTO BY SPC. JEFFREY ALEXANDER.*

JUNE

SAIC's profits grow. The company attributes the rise to its support for work in Iraq, Kuwait, and Afghanistan, particularly its logistics work on MRAP vehicles.

IDEAS, INC.

The company's expanded and unparalleled expertise in the defense and security arena is due in part to several strategic acquisitions as well as its own growth trajectory. For example, in 1994, SAIC acquired the government unit of Ideas, Inc., which provided complex telecommunications products and services to Department of Defense customers.

CEO J. Robert Beyster said at the time:

We are pleased to be able to add the proven technical capabilities and outstanding professional reputation of Ideas to our SAIC staff. This organization complements our existing business, and we believe it will continue to prosper as part of our company.

addressing possible regional conflicts, as well as keeping nuclear, biological, and chemical weapons out of the hands of unstable or adversarial regimes.

The Soviet Union's dissolution left nuclear weapons scattered throughout many of the country's former republics. There was concern that these weapons could be sold to rogue states such as North Korea, Iraq, and Iran, or a terrorist organization. Russia requested help to secure the weapons.

Through the Nunn–Lugar Cooperative Threat Reduction Program, the DoD reached out to SAIC to assist in denuclearizing the former Soviet

2008

JULY

The U.S. Air Force awards a contract worth some $900 million to several defense firms, including SAIC, to offer services to the Pentagon department that controls nuclear weapons.

2009

MAY

SAIC receives a Marine Corps contract worth up to $96 million for a program that responds to biological, chemical, and other attacks.

2011

CREDIT: U.S. NAVY PHOTO BY MASS COMMUNICATION SPECIALIST 2ND CLASS SCOTT FENAROLI/RELEASED.*

MAY 2

Under the cover of darkness, U.S. Navy SEALs infiltrate a compound in Abbottabad, Pakistan, and kill Osama bin Laden, leader of al-Qaeda and mastermind of the terrorist attacks in New York, Pennsylvania, and Washington, D.C., nearly a decade earlier.

*The appearance of U.S. Department of Defense (DoD) visual information does not imply or constitute DoD endorsement.

Leidos maintains the U.S. government's information infrastructure, which includes managing the White House hotlines. *(Photo on Visual Hunt.)*

republics. SAIC's experience and history working for the Defense Nuclear Agency and Los Alamos played a big role in SAIC winning the job, which included deactivating and moving warheads, destroying missiles, and using environmentally proper methods to dispose of rocket fuel. The work proved to be a pivotal example of how SAIC could serve the country and maintain its relevance as new threats emerged and government priorities shifted.

One of the reasons Leidos has been able to develop defense and intelligence solutions for many of the world's most critical problems is a result of the company's continuously expanding spectrum of capabilities. While expansion into new areas of work is often triggered by the needs of customers, the "you are only bound by your ideas" culture of Leidos motivates employees to think beyond the goals of a project, and further, beyond the present limitations within their area of expertise. "What we have is the ability to be agnostic," said retired U.S. Air Force General John Jumper, who served as CEO during SAIC's transition to Leidos in 2013. "That means we are truly going to go search for the right solution for our customers, and it doesn't matter where that solution comes from or how we put it together."

When it comes to thinking beyond limitations, retired U.S. Army General Brian Keller, who currently serves as vice president and account executive for Army Strategic Accounts, offered his insight on the company's mission:

> *If you are passionate about growing professionally and making contributions to our nation's security in some of the toughest challenges that we have as a nation, then you want to come to a company like Leidos, because that is our forté. We know and understand our customer. We're dedicated to ensuring that what they need to support our nation and win wars and make our world safer and make our world more productive, is exactly what we deliver.*

Securing the Lines of Communication

One key Leidos contract in the communications arena is with the Defense Information Systems Agency (DISA) through its Global Systems Management Operations (GSM-O). DISA is the single organization that oversees the entire U.S. government information infrastructure, managing both classified and unclassified communication systems. The broad scope of DISA includes maintaining communications within 4,300 locations, reaching more than 90 nations.

One of DISA's most visible roles is in support of the Executive Branch. Through its work with the White House Communications Agency, DISA manages what is popularly known as the "hotline" system that allows the president and other leaders within the government and the military to communicate with leaders from other nations. The first of these hotlines connected the Pentagon with the Kremlin during the Cold War through a teletype system that became operational on August 30, 1963.

Today, there are more than 100 hotlines between the United States and the world's leadership, both in the Executive Branch and within the DoD and the State Department. DISA negotiates, maintains, and operates the hotlines, while Leidos maintains the global network itself as well as managing the cybersecurity.

"Information technology progresses so rapidly, it's hard to keep up," said retired U.S. Air Force Lieutenant General Charles Croom, the senior vice president and the director of strategic account executives at Leidos, who is involved in much of the company's GSM-O work. "It's hard to keep up with your own personal cellphone, but now imagine a global network of three and a half million users and trying to keep that modernized."

The next steps Leidos is taking in the modernization of DISA's global communications network includes downsizing the manpower resources needed to run the system, particularly overseas, by centralizing and automating the technology. The operational convergence of the network will ultimately serve to improve efficiency, accuracy, and security for the customer.

The diverse opportunities within the IT field make the company an ideal workplace for those who are highly skilled in the field of information technology and cybersecurity.

As for those individuals who are highly skilled in the field of information technology and cybersecurity, General Croom believes there is nowhere better than Leidos to make a career:

The SAI Technology (SAIT) unit developed the Lightweight Computer Unit (LCU) for the U.S. Army. The rugged laptop was designed for soldiers to use in the field.

We're on the edge of technology. If you want to be in a place where there's rapid change, where there's opportunity for advancement, where the work is exciting, where you're doing things that support government efforts like DISA—the executive leadership, the president, the national commanders—this is where it's happening. Leidos is right there at the front of that as the largest provider of IT services to the federal government.

The LCU is Born

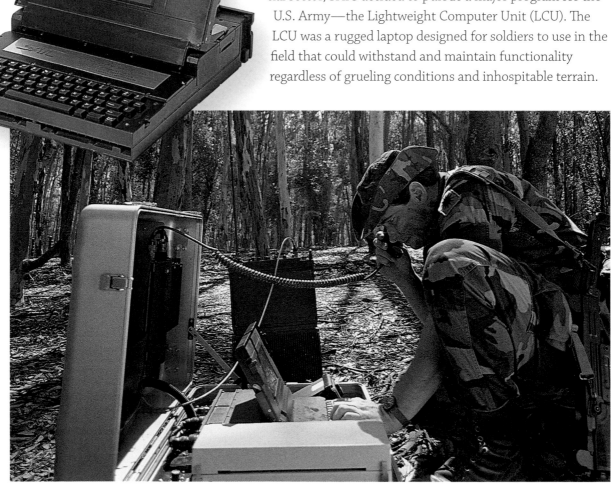

Although Leidos is known as a service provider, the company has also created several products over the years to keep our government, and those who work for it, safe and secure. Using experience gained while developing products for the commercial sector, SAIC decided to pursue a major program for the U.S. Army—the Lightweight Computer Unit (LCU). The LCU was a rugged laptop designed for soldiers to use in the field that could withstand and maintain functionality regardless of grueling conditions and inhospitable terrain.

QUICK PLANNING IN TIMES OF NEED

Although many people think of govern-ment contracts as slow-moving programs with long negotiations, when the world is in a time of need, they can move quickly and efficiently. One such case was immediately after September 11, 2001, when the company was called upon to create a security system in just 48 hours. SAIC invested more than $2 million in the project without a formal contract, "just a promise from a customer, a whole lot of patriotism, and a belief in our technology," said former SAIC Vice President Steve Rizzi to CEO J. Robert Beyster.

The laptop was created by the SAI Technology (SAIT) unit, which became a profitable segment after the LCU's introduction. With the success of the LCU, SAIT pitched this new rugged, field-ready equipment to other military services and businesses in the commercial sector such as the automotive and oil industries. While the LCU was a popular product with the armed services, it never reached the same level of success in the commercial industry. SAIT met a similar fate. "Eventually, we decided that SAIT was not generating the return that we needed to keep it viable, so in 1997, we sold SAIT to Litton Industries," Beyster later wrote.

A Stryker lies on its side after surviving a buried IED blast in 2007. The Stryker was recovered and protected its soldiers on more missions until another bomb finally put it out of action. *(Photo courtesy of C-52 of 3/2 Stryker Brigade Combat Team.)**

Lessons from the Battlefield

Leidos has always relied on experience and history when expanding into new fields or bidding on new projects. While time was often on the company's side, the wars in Afghanistan and Iraq would demand quick and effective solutions to combat challenges. Jim Cantor, chief engineer of the national security sector at Leidos, recalled the company's mindset at the time:

> *The needs were too urgent, and the missions too critical, for us to go through our standard acquisition cycle again. We had to act quickly, so the mindset was "give me what you've got, let's get it out there, and see if it can help."*

Above and Below:
SAIC installed and tested the electronics for 30,000 Mine Resistant Ambush Protected (MRAP) vehicles in Charleston, South Carolina, to be sent to Afghanistan and Iraq.

U.S. soldiers were equipped with the latest and most advanced weaponry and armor, but the conflicts in Iraq and Afghanistan introduced a new weapon the military was not prepared for—improvised explosive devices (IEDs). These homemade bombs would be responsible for more American casualties than any other weapon. Two-thirds of Americans killed or wounded in combat in the Iraq and Afghanistan wars were victims of IEDs planted in the ground, placed in vehicles or buildings, worn as suicide vests, or loaded into suicide vehicles. It was imperative that SAIC transition new technologies to the battlefield as quickly as possible to protect soldiers and national security.

Dr. John J. Fratamico Jr., chief technology officer at Leidos, explained:

We were losing a lot of Americans to IEDs and the threat from that. So developing rapid solutions for change detection and finding IEDs and precursors to them were important for us. We rapidly deployed a number of advanced technologies with electro-optics, hyper-spectral imagery, change detection methods, and so forth, and what I'm proud of is that we were able to get those systems into theater very quickly with appropriately trained crews and a very, very high safety record.

One example of those IED projects was the Mine Resistant Ambush Protected (MRAP) vehicle. Soldiers traveling or on patrol risked attacks from rocket-propelled grenades, explosively formed penetrators, underbody mines, small arms fire threats, and IEDs. Initially, the U.S. Army responded by improvising protections such as metal caging around the exterior of vehicles to cause incoming warheads to prematurely detonate. But most of the efforts failed.

MRAPs proved to be twice as effective as M1 Abrams tanks and more than three times as effective as the armored Humvees for protecting vehicle passengers. MRAPs were designed with a V-shaped hull to deflect explosions upward and

TAKING PRIDE IN SAVING MILITARY LIVES

In 2009, the number one killer of troops and civilians in Iraq was not gunfire, but improvised explosive devices (IEDs), more commonly referred to as roadside bombs. That year, former Secretary of the U.S. Air Force Deborah Lee James, who had become an SAIC business unit general manager, learned that the company would be a driving force devoted to mitigating the devastating impacts of IEDs.

James, who eventually rose to become president of the SAIC Technology and Engineering Sector, learned that the company was going to work on a project known as MRAP (Mine Resistant Ambush Protected) vehicle. She later recalled:

There was this very urgent requirement that suddenly became DoD's number one program—MRAP. It was basically heavied-up vehicles that could transport the troops, and it had a different type of design that made it more blast resistant. This was imperative, because it was work tied to immediate lifesaving. There were different companies that manufactured these MRAPs, but all 30,000 of them that were produced by industry came to Charleston, South Carolina, where we—the SAIC workforce working under a division of the Navy—did all the command
and control, integration, and testing. We made sure that the different electronics worked properly together, that one system didn't jam another. We tested everything and then pushed them out in an assembly line fashion to either the Charleston seaport or to the Air Force base there, to be taken over to Iraq.

According to James, the project prompted SAIC to hire hundreds of people in a short period to crank out 50 MRAPs a day. Site visitors included the secretary of defense and U.S. senators as well as the SAIC board and CEO, who came to review the progress and show support for the mission at hand.

"It was high visibility, and it was a source of great pride. And in terms of the military and business leaders who came to speak with the workforce, the most powerful speakers, with all due respect, were a sergeant and a private in the Army," said James. "They essentially told the story of how they were in one of these vehicles in Iraq, and it hit a mine. They talked about that experience and the fact that they walked away from it—they lived. And hundreds of us, men and women, our entire workforce, listened to these young soldiers—they were all crying. It was a very touching moment."

away from the troop compartment. "So now, when an armored vehicle would hit a mine on the roadside, the troops inside might get shook up, but they wouldn't die," explained Deborah Lee James, former secretary of the Air Force and former president of SAIC's technology and engineering sector. Several companies manufactured the MRAPs, but SAIC was responsible for installing the electronics into each of the vehicles and making sure various electronic devices worked in unison.

Leidos did not receive public accolades for all the work the company performed for the military in Iraq and Afghanistan, but success was a reward in itself. "It's classified, and you can't always talk about the breadth and depth of everything your company does, but you can be very proud of what you do at a national and even a global level," said Cantor.

Contract Logistics Support

The Afghan Contractor Logistics Support (CLS) program combined five independent programs supporting the U.S. Government and Afghan Air Force since 2009. It is an amalgamation of several aviation training disciplines into one large program—Rotary- and Fixed-Wing Aircraft Maintenance, Aviation Logistics and Procurement, Rotary- and Fixed-Wing Pilot Training, and Language and Operations Support. The program provides a textbook example of partnering contractually with the United States government while operationally supporting the U.S. Air Force and Army, working "shoulder to shoulder" with a foreign military in an austere environment. The program goal is to transition all aviation responsibilities to the Afghan Air Force by building a military capability that can sustain and defend itself against all enemies.

Above: A recently repaired Afghan Air Force Mi-17 inside a hangar February 18, 2018, at Kandahar Air Wing, Afghanistan.
*(U.S. Air Force photo by Staff Sgt. Jared J. Duhon.)**

Right: Afghan crews manage and execute all aspects of routine maintenance and flight operations for the Mi-17 helicopter at Kandahar Airfield, Afghanistan.
*(U.S. Air Force photo by Staff Sgt. Alexander W. Riedel.)**

Since the program's inception, Leidos has provided all services, supplies, materials, equipment, and personnel necessary to perform CLS for approximately 80 aircraft maintained by the Afghan Air Force. These services included training Afghan pilots to fly, instructing technicians to maintain aircraft, incorporating demand-based logistics, preparing controllers to direct flight schedules, and teaching the English language. The company's program support has met technical and cultural challenges and helped USG agencies meet U.S. and North Atlantic Treaty Organization (NATO) objectives along a difficult path leading to Afghan military and civil self-sufficiency. The program was designed to integrate flight operations, planning, right-sized inventory management, maintenance phase flow, and integrated training support to deliver mission capability and provide flexibility to meet the Afghan Air Force mission to stabilize, optimize, and transform.

Major General L. Neil Thurgood, deputy commander of the Combined Security Transition Command-Afghanistan stated:

The decisive air platform for the support of operations in Afghanistan remains rotary-wing aviation. Fix-wing assets play a critical role, remaining in the focused area of attack and logistics support, which is a growing capability. Rotary-wing assault, movement, logistics, and attack are the most demanded resources by the Afghan Corps Commanders. The support and maintenance of the precious rotary-wing resources are the key to their operational success. Leidos, as the primary lead for rotary-wing maintenance of the Mi-17 for the Afghan Air Force, is unmatched globally in their success. With rotary-wing assets spread across four primary and numerous secondary locations, Leidos' ability to plan, coordinate, and execute sustainment operations in concert with our Afghan Air Force partners is the key enabler. The on-ground team, led by Mark Funk, is simply world-class.

The Afghan Air Force conducts night flight training exercises with the Mi-17 helicopter at Kandahar Airfield, Afghanistan.
(U.S. Army photo by Spc. Jaerett Engeseth.)*

INTERCONNECTING NATO

DoD PHOTO BY JIM GARAMONE.*

When the North Atlantic Treaty Organization (NATO) announced plans to build a brand new state-of-the-art headquarters across the street from its old headquarters in Brussels, Belgium, Leidos was called on to develop, implement, and maintain all of the IT capabilities for the new facility. The project, named the Active Network Infrastructure Program (ANWI), would implement a full set of capabilities, from mobility, voice and video, desktop, server, virtualization, and networking into the facility. The task of designing and building the IT system from the ground up for one of the most highly targeted organizations by enemy states would once

DoD PHOTO BY JIM GARAMONE.*

again put the company's cybersecurity capabilities on an international stage.

Adding to the project's high level of complexity was the collaborative coordination involved in working on what would need to be one of the most secure facilities in the world. More than 1,400 security cameras have been installed across the complex.

"Those were being implemented by a separate program and a separate contractor, yet those cameras and the data had to ride over the network we were building," said Daniel Voce, vice president of Leidos enterprise and cyber solutions business, who helped guide the ANWI project. "So you can imagine a coordination effort between all the different contractors in the building. And while we were implementing our network, others were using the network. So that in and of itself was an engineering challenge that, I think, required a company like Leidos to address."

If the significant exposure, magnitude, complexity, and coordination with other contractors involved in the project did not present enough of a challenge, the hard deadline added yet another layer of pressure and difficulty. Most of the work on the NATO facility, especially in the area of IT, needed to be completed and functional before the 2017 Brussels Summit, as Voce explained:

We were still building out the IT system, yet this major international conference was happening in the building with all the leaders of the NATO countries, to include President Trump. So you're trying to make sure that's a success while you're still in the process of building out the IT equipment. Those security cameras had to be working when those world leaders were on the campus. It was a no-fail mission. And it was something that went very successfully.

DoD PHOTO BY JIM GARAMONE.*

Ensuring a Safer Future

By the time the country entered the new millennium, SAIC was considered a leader in defense contracting, which led to a contract helping to create a system that would ensure shipping containers entering American ports were safe in the wake of the September 11th terrorist attacks. The Integrated Container Inspection System (ICIS) swiftly scanned moving, closed containers to evaluate whether any radiation or weapons of mass destruction were inside, enabling customs officials to quickly identify high-risk containers.

Among other projects in the late 2000s, the company won a contract from the Army to improve the Advanced Night Vision System for urban environments. Additionally, SAIC was awarded a project to help the Pentagon replicate a dog's sniffing ability to detect bombs as part of the Defense Advanced Research Projects Agency's (DARPA) RealNose program.

Presently, Leidos provides a diverse portfolio of systems, solutions, and services covering air, land, sea, space, and cyberspace for customers worldwide. The company currently provides solutions for enterprise and mission IT, large-scale intelligence systems, command and control, geospatial and data analytics, cybersecurity, logistics, training, and intelligence analysis and operations support. "Everything that Leidos specializes in—its technical core competencies—are technologies and capabilities that will carry into the future for decades to come," said Reardon. "You're going to find that the big missile systems, the aviation systems, the satellite systems, have much more reliance and connectivity

SAIC created a system to ensure that shipping containers that entered American ports were safe.

Left: SAIC won a contract from the U.S. Army to improve the Advanced Night Vision System for urban environments. Pictured are American soldiers providing security at the scene of fighting in Al-Fadhel in eastern Baghdad, Iraq, March 2009. *(Detail from U.S. Army photo/Flickr, https:// creativecommons.org/ licenses/by/4.0/.)**

with capabilities on the ground, and that's information technology; it's cyber; it's big data; it's enterprise IT modernization. Everything has become networked and interconnected."

For those who are looking to make a career at Leidos, Reardon described what made the work rewarding:

> *The ability to work on national security issues and really make a difference for our nation is what makes coming into work every day much more compelling and interesting than it would for other reasons. If you want to work on the next internet e-mail application or a browser search capability, that's fantastic. If you enjoy that, I'm not putting it down. But for me, it's much more interesting to work on a capability that's going to help us stop Iran from developing a nuclear weapon or stop Syria from deploying chemical weapons. You can come up with an infinite list. But it's that extra national security punch of knowing that what you're doing is really making a difference for the nation, that I find really compelling and interesting.*

Below: The company was awarded a contract for the Defense Advanced Research Projects Agency's (DARPA) RealNose program. The goal of the program was to create a sensor with the olfactory abilities of a dog to detect explosive, chemical, and biological weapons.

Though Leidos is not a widely-recognized name, the public can sleep easier at night because the men and women at Leidos are constantly working to develop innovative solutions to keep the world safe. ■

CHAPTER SIX

ADVANCED SOLUTIONS

Airborne ISR; maritime autonomous systems; sensors, collection, and phenomenology; command and control; training systems; electronic warfare systems; and key management—those are the areas our Advanced Solutions will continue to invest in.

Michael Chagnon
PRESIDENT OF THE LEIDOS ADVANCED SOLUTIONS BUSINESS

A NUMBER OF COMPANIES CAN TAKE A TECHNOLOGICAL system and keep it running, but when it comes to innovation, thought leadership is often the key ingredient that inspires scientific discovery and technological development. Within the Leidos approach to advanced solutions, a heavy emphasis on thought leadership has translated numerous discoveries and developments into actionable solutions that have enhanced the areas of reconnaissance, autonomy, data analytics, surveillance, and other forms of intelligence gathering. From mapping the ocean with unmanned surface vehicles to designing adaptive combat training simulators, the team delivers science and technology solutions tailored to the specific needs of its customers.

This work within Leidos serves as the company's research and development arm and requires the brightest minds in the industry. Teams are constantly working on leading-edge innovations that help shape the portfolios within each area of the company.

"There are many opportunities for innovators in our area of work," said Michael Chagnon, president of the advanced solutions business for Leidos. "You could be building sensors, re-engineering an aircraft with sensors, or developing operational software that the Army uses for fire control management. The sky is the limit."

Opposite: Leidos has supported multiple U.S. military missions, including Operations Allied Force, Enduring Freedom, Iraqi Freedom, and New Dawn.

Above: President Michael Chagnon leads the company's advanced solutions work.

Right: The Leidos Next Generation: Remotely Piloted Aircraft (RPA) Operations Center offers 24-hour operations and mission support of unmanned systems.

Chagnon, with the company since 1988, sees Leidos poised to become the largest defense contractor in the nation within the next decade. He believes the company will attain that designation largely due to the Leidos emphasis on collaboration, which is a core component in day-to-day operations. "We are constantly looking for ways to collaborate instead of operating in silos," said Chagnon. "As we continue to enhance the understanding across the company of all the different things that we do, we will further our ability to work efficiently to deliver best-in-class solutions to meet our customers' most challenging requirements."

1990

Sailors begin advanced training in classrooms and real-life simulations under a U.S. Navy contract with SAIC.

1999

Work begins on the Army's OneSAF modeling and simulation-based training systems that mimic battlefield and attack conditions.

2006

SAIC is awarded the NATO Active Layered Theater Ballistic Missile Defense (ALTBMD) SE&I contract, leading a consortium of ten companies representing six different countries. Successfully executed, this program continues to prime its successor program (BMD SE&I), at a cumulative value of $231.2 million.

2007

The Angel Fire electro-optical sensor program was awarded and deployed to outfit warfighters with advanced sensor systems.

Airborne Systems Integration

When airborne ISR data is critical to the success of a mission, the U.S. military calls on Leidos for support. The Airborne Integration and Ground Processing Systems areas within the company specialize in the development, operations, and maintenance of manned and unmanned Intelligence, Surveillance, and Reconnaissance (ISR) systems. These systems support the warfighter in combat zones worldwide through the use of advanced sensors to collect, process, exploit, and disseminate mission-essential data.

Over the past 15 years, Leidos has designed and deployed 16 different ISR aircraft configurations and deployed more than 60 aircraft to support U.S. troops. In 2012 during the peak of the Global War on Terrorism, Leidos operated and maintained 25 ISR aircraft in Afghanistan.

Leidos-owned aircraft equipped with the HR3DGI sensor system collect and process sensor data used to generate unclassified, high resolution, 3-D geospatial information.

2010

SAIC develops the first integrated simulators for the Black Hawk and Chinook helicopters, saving costly flight time and providing intricate training simulations for all crew members.

2010

The U.S. military relies on the SAIC-supported Night Eagle program to detect IEDs at night in Afghanistan from aircraft.

2011

Recognizing the need to rapidly and continuously migrate legacy Command and Control systems, SAIC initiates a multi-year $20 million internal R&D effort to develop a framework (later known as LEAF) that would serve as a discriminator in $1 billion in awards across the DoD, Health and Civil domains over the next 10 years.

2012

SAIC becomes one of seven Primes awarded the $249 million C2 Applications and Information Services Development (C2AD) ID/IQ Contract that becomes the proverbial "foot in the door" as SAIC and then Leidos begin to unseat incumbent OEMs in the DoD C2 domain.

Bill Kraus, former operations manager of Airborne Integration and Ground Processing Systems, said of the operation's beginnings:

> *When SAIC started in the Airborne ISR business, we had a few pro-*
> *gram managers and engineers, and a majority of work was subcontracted.*
> *As our airborne ISR work increased, over the past 10 years, we grew*
> *our in-house staff and capabilities in areas of engineering, airborne*
> *system operators, logistics, and maintenance. We are evolving from*
> *leasing airplanes to now being in the position that we own a fleet of*
> *six aircraft and we can also modify, upgrade, and operate government-*
> *owned airplanes.*

In 2015, the U.S. Army awarded Leidos a contract related to the Airborne Reconnaissance Low-Enhanced (ARL-E) fleet. Leidos handles design, engineering, and technical and logistical support of the fixed-wing ARL-E aircraft, which uses multiple onboard sensors to track ground targets. The first aircraft entered operational testing in late 2018, and Leidos is under contract to deliver the second and third ARL-E systems, with an anticipated fleet size of nine aircraft.

After the announcement of the contract, Dr. Loren Thompson, chief operating officer of the Lexington Institute, a national security think tank in Arlington, Virginia, told the *Washington Business Journal*:

> *The focus of Leidos' strategy is on high-end technical services and that*
> *includes the sustainment of specialized military aircraft equipped with*
> *sophisticated electronics. Leidos can do this better than any normal aircraft*
> *maintenance operation would, and it probably brings unique skills to the*
> *table in terms of reconnaissance and surveillance technology.*

2014

Leidos takes over several facets of the development of the new Combatant Craft Medium Mk1 (CCM Mk1).

2015

Leidos begins design, engineering, technical, and logistical support for the U.S. Army's Airborne Reconnaissance Low-Enhanced (ARL-E) fleet under a $661.8 million contract.

2016

Leidos takes over development of the Common Driver Trainer (CDT) system, which trains crew members in conditions too dangerous to simulate in real life.

2016

Leidos wins the Air Execution Information Services (AXIS) task order under the C2AD contract that firmly establishes Leidos as a true player in the DoD C2 realm.

Following the ARL-E program, Leidos was awarded a contract to develop the High-Resolution 3-D Geospatial Information (HR3DGI) sensor system. Deployed on a variety of manned and unmanned aircraft, this platform-agnostic system collects and processes sensor data to generate unclassified, high-resolution, 3-D geospatial mapping information that is critical for the warfighter in theater.

The company's extensive work in airborne systems has evolved from Quick Reaction Capability (QRC) programs in the early 2000s to winning the Army's ARL-E program in 2015. Over this period, Leidos built a strong team of engineers, operations, and maintenance personnel and matured its processes, allowing the company to win the ARL-E contract and to acquire and modify aircraft to support the Army's HR3DGI mission. Leidos also continues to support and upgrade the Army's Night Eagle and Saturn Arch QRC ISR aircraft with new sensors and processing and exploitation hardware and software.

Fixed-wing Saturn Arch aircraft carrying remote sensing hardware and software during test flights in Nevada.

2016

The U.S. Army's Geospatial Center awards Leidos a $777 million contract to support the High-Resolution, 3-D Geospatial Information program, or HR3DGI.

2017

The Martin H. Harris Chapter of the Air Force Association recognizes the Leidos Remotely Piloted Aircraft (RPA) Operations Center for outstanding current/future armed unmanned aerial vehicle (UAV) technology.

2017

Leidos begins developing the U.S. Army's Synthetic Environment Core (SE Core) Common Virtual Environment Management (CVEM) program.

2017

Leidos is awarded a $98 million contract to deliver the next iteration of the U.S. Army's Advanced Field Artillery Tactical Data System, unseating Raytheon as the long-time incumbent on the program.

When it comes to winning such contracts, Leidos bids best-value solutions based on a deep understanding of its customer's mission requirements and available technologies, combined with an efficient and cost-effective approach, to provide exceptional products and service. As Kraus described:

> *Understanding our customer and understanding the warfighters' needs were, and continue to be, critical to our success. We understood applying current and emerging sensor, processing, and exploitation technologies to directly support the warfighter. Our objective was focusing on mission success by ensuring deployed aircraft maximized operational availability, and we remain responsive to changing mission requirements. We work with our customer and the warfighter to upgrade systems to increase effectiveness. Our success over the past 10 years proves that focusing on the customer and the end-user is the right business model for customer satisfaction and meeting company objectives.*

After 15 years, Leidos ISR-equipped aircraft systems have flown thousands of hours in combat zones around the world and continue to specialize in gathering mission-critical information for the tactical customer. Leidos has integrated, deployed, operated, and maintained more than 60 ISR aircraft through the years. Building on its employees' knowledge, capabilities, and expertise in this area, Leidos now owns and operates seven ISR aircraft today.

Maritime Solutions

Leidos is responsible for developing several key portions of the Combatant Craft Medium Mk1 (CCM Mk1) project.

In addition to the company's work with Airborne ISR systems, Leidos has decades of experience developing and maintaining maritime systems and instruments, including autonomous craft and high-fidelity ocean modeling.

Among these endeavors was a project for the U.S. Special Operations Command (USSOCOM) to help develop the Combatant Craft Medium Mk1 (CCM Mk1), a long-range watercraft that can travel at 52 knots to relay intelligence information to warfighters. Leidos would produce several portions of the program, including testing the tactical computing systems and logistical support and upgrades.

Perhaps the craft that best exemplifies the Leidos work in the maritime arena is the *Sea Hunter* trimaran. Developed for the Defense Advanced Research Projects Agency's (DARPA) Anti-Submarine

SEA HUNTER

The U.S. Defense Advanced Research Projects Agency (DARPA) contracted with Leidos in 2012 to support a submarine-tracking program. The Anti-Submarine Warfare Continuous Trail Unmanned Vessel (ACTUV) is an autonomous unmanned ship that can cover thousands of nautical miles in the ocean for months on end.

At a ceremony in April 2016, Leidos christened the ACTUV ship *Sea Hunter*. Testing that followed showed the 132-foot trimaran could execute a multi-waypoint mission without an actual person directing the course or changing speeds. "The operational testing is designed to showcase the unprecedented capabilities that this type of unmanned vessel could offer our military forces," said Michael Chagnon, president of the advanced solutions unit at Leidos. *Sea Hunter*'s Remote Supervisory Control Station (RSCS)

allows it to accept new tasks from remote locations. Testing continued through Fall 2017 with funding provided in part from the Office of Naval Research (ONR). Chagnon said *Sea Hunter* "has been a phenomenal accomplishment for the company" and represents "dramatic" advances in maritime autonomy.

Leidos continues to conduct testing off the coast of Southern California to maintain the vessel's collision regulations and participate in even more complex tests. "It was originally designed to be an anti-submarine warfare asset, but they're looking at other potential missions, including countermeasures, surveys, deception, or logistics," said Chagnon. "What we would like to get maritime autonomous vessels involved in is what we call the dull, the dirty, and the dangerous, to take the warfighter out of harm's way."

Warfare Continuous Trail Unmanned Vessel (ACTUV) program, *Sea Hunter* is one of several unmanned vehicles developed by the company and a symbol of what autonomous technology can accomplish at sea. "One of the reasons we won the Sea Hunter contract is because we spent a lot of time thinking about how to actually do this mission instead of just giving them what we thought they wanted to hear," said retired U.S. Navy Rear Admiral Nevin Carr, who serves as a Leidos vice president and as the U.S. Navy strategic account executive. "We did a lot of analysis and we came up with a very elegant naval architectural solution that was efficient and could do the mission in very bad weather, and for long periods of time. DARPA saw the value in that and awarded us the contract, even though we were not the biggest competitor by far."

Rus Cook, the senior program manager of the Sea Hunter project at Leidos, described the program's initial goals:

Leidos has developed a variety of programs and systems to help the U.S. Navy obtain and decipher maritime data.

The original mission was anti-submarine warfare, where we would have this huge sonar in our keel, we'd go out, and we'd get to an area where we'd be told: "We think there's an enemy submarine in the area." We'd go to that area, search it, find it, and then just trail it. More than likely, they would hear us and know that we were following them, and then leave wherever they're not supposed to be.

In October 2017, *GCN*, an industry publication, recognized *Sea Hunter*'s contributions to maritime innovation at its yearly digIT Awards event, which recognizes transformative technologies. DARPA and Leidos won the award in the Robotics, Automation & Unmanned Systems category for its work on the Sea Hunter project.

The vessel not only has the ability to travel for months at sea without crew members, but *Sea Hunter* creates a new advantage for the U.S. military in surveillance and anti-submarine warfare. "Our goal is to arm the Navy with a fleet of *Sea Hunters*," said Cook. "In a perfect world, we would be building ten a year and they would be going out and doing multiple things. There would be a variant for different missions, and those I can't really talk about."

Continuing its work to develop and test new capabilities that will offer customers every advantage in the surging field of auton-

SURVEY ANALYSIS AND AREA BASED EDITOR (SABER)

Leidos has been at the forefront of hydrographic, oceanographic, and geophysical surveys in coastal areas around the world since the 1970s. The company still offers cost-effective marine data and management support to its customers through products like its Survey Analysis and Area Based Editor (SABER).

SABER processes the massive amount of data involved with hydrographic surveys and then provides 3-D displays. The new SABER 5.0 includes Automated Contact Detection (ACD) capability, which can detect objects protruding from the sea floor. It works in three phases: initial detection from side-scan sonar data; determining if detection is legitimate or false using a trained neural network; and a review from a human analyst. After the data is processed, SABER can cull enormous volumes of information. The system can then generate color-coded bathymetry grids and sonar imagery mosaics within the latest standards in hydrography.

omy, Leidos demonstrated new unmanned maritime capabilities during the U.S. Navy's Advanced Naval Technology Exercise (ANTX) in 2017. The company's autonomous test vessel, R/V *Pathfinder*, collected data in multiple locations. *Pathfinder* surveyed the ocean floor off Panama City, Florida, and launched and recovered its own unmanned underwater vehicle. "Our participation at ANTX enables us to show our innovative autonomous technology directly to our Navy and government customers," said Carr.

Chuck Fralick, the maritime solutions architect for Advanced Solutions, added:

> *If we can send large UVs with small unmanned underwater vehicles that can go off and do their missions, that means we can greatly expand our resources in the Navy without increasing the manned footprint. If you want to do a sweep of a minefield, you don't want to put people into that minefield, because that's hazardous. If we can take those dull, dirty, and dangerous jobs and assign them to autonomous platforms and take the human out of the loop, we can save lives. We also believe, and I think there's significant evidence to show, that if you do it right, you can greatly reduce the cost to the government. Those are the types of things we're doing with autonomy.*

Leidos has provided research and development for DARPA's deep ocean sensors, called TRAPS. *(Photo by Brian Hamburg.)*

In addition to the company's maritime autonomy projects, Leidos has also developed several projects in the domain of underwater Sensors, Collection, and Phenomenology (SCP). "In general, SCP is the art of understanding the world through the physics of sensing, and how you might perceive those signals," said Tim Cunningham, Leidos director of business development in Sensors, Collection, and Phenomenology. "Next is the mathematics of processing what you can actually measure with a sensor to eliminate the noise and background environmental fluctuations. Finally, it involves getting the pure signal and understanding the originating physical phenomena behind that signal. This competency area also extends to how Leidos implements multiple sensor modalities and integrates collection systems to meet demanding customer needs."

In 2014, DARPA awarded Leidos a contract to develop deep ocean sensors that came under the umbrella of the agency's Distributed Agile Submarine Hunter (DASH) program. A component of the DASH program developed by Leidos is the Transformational Reliable Acoustic Path System (TRAPS), a fixed passive sonar node designed to achieve large area coverage by exploiting advantages of operating from the deep seafloor. Carr explained TRAPS' functionality when compared to Sonar:

> *Think about a refrigerator-sized box that you can literally throw over the side of the ship; it sinks to the bottom and on its way down, it pays out its hydrophone arrays. When it lands on the ocean bottom, the reliable acoustic path is what you get in certain underwater geometries when you're on the bottom looking up. Right now, all the sonars on our ships are on the surface looking down. When you do that, it's like looking down into an echo chamber. But when you're on the bottom looking up, you don't have that same bottom echo or reverberation and it gives you an acoustic advantage.*

Advanced Surveillance

Adding to its innovative work in the areas of autonomy and SCP at sea, Leidos has also developed real-world applications of these surveillance technologies for use in other environments. In the area of autonomy, engineers designed an advanced robotic device that could be utilized during hostage standoff situations. "Imagine if criminals or terrorists have a hostage in a building—you don't want your law enforcement or paramilitary or military troops storming rooms because they can get hostages killed, or themselves killed," said Fralick, who added:

> *We're always looking for ways that we can penetrate a room and see what's going on inside without endangering anybody. So we looked at autonomizing thin snake-like devices that can move through rooms very quietly and discreetly, and we had cameras mounted on them.*

While various types of autonomous devices can be used to detect the location of a threat within a physical space, the use of sensors, collection, and specifically, the science of phenomenology, takes surveillance many steps further by examining all of the phenomena that would indicate the existence of a threat. "People breathe, so one phenomenon is that their chest might expand and contract at their breathing rate," said Cunningham. "Human beings also emit modest amounts of heat. They emit moisture through perspiration and respiration, so they typically add humidity to an environment. These are ways we might detect a person in a building remotely. When we consider the range of phenomena that an object of interest generates, we're engaging in phenomenology."

One of the company's advanced surveillance technologies is a situational awareness tool named Integrated Building Interior Surveillance System (IBISS). The system uses through-wall radar sensors to reconstruct 3-D floor plans of building interiors, detect and track occupants, and display the composite dynamic interior situation in an interactive 3-D display.

Through the use of frequencies or radar, experts in phenomenology are able to "see" through walls through the detection of various signals. And while there may be environments that consist of other phenomena that might mask a signal or create interference, such as air currents, if all of the data is processed correctly, phenomenology experts can determine "true" detections from false alarms.

When it comes to the application of phenomenology in theater, Cunningham provided a real world example:

> *Let's say you're a technical battlefield commander, and you're faced with an enemy who is positioned in heavy woods. You know they have combat ground vehicles, but you don't know exactly how many, what type, and where they are. If you were to fly over that wooded area, and you had a sensor that enabled you to detect all the big metal objects, you would look at that data and know where those objects are. But you'd also like to understand what class of object they are, whether each one of them is a tank, Jeep, artillery piece, or command post. Now let's say that I understand which of those big metal things are tanks, Humvees, command posts, and artillery pieces. Identification would go further and say, "This tank is a Russian T38," or "That command post is for an anti-air battery," or "This is a Humvee, and it's got some really interesting enclosure on the back of it." Now we're starting to identify for the commander exactly what threat he's facing in this environment so that he can respond to it appropriately in real time.*

Leidos developed the Army's OneSAF program, open-sourced software, which can be reprogrammed to create new simulated combat situations.

Advanced Training Solutions

Leidos has a long history of helping the Armed Forces ensure that soldiers in combat zones are ready for anything. Starting in 1990, then-SAIC provided advanced training simulations for U.S. Navy sailors. These signature-based trainers provided classroom and real-life simulations meant to represent an at-sea environment.

Two years later, DARPA awarded SAIC the contract to develop its Semi-Automated Forces program, which would be made up of systems that combine computer generation, simulators, and live training capabilities to mimic realistic battlefield and attack conditions. The program was spearheaded by James Shiflett, a senior business development executive at Leidos. Shiflett described his early days working on semi-automated forces with the company:

The OneSAF program reduced redundant training software by adjusting to new real-life challenges for simulated combat situations.

I joined SAIC because they didn't know a lot about the topic of semi-automated forces when the contract was awarded in 1992, but they were willing to learn and listen, and to adjust based upon new information. They had very bright people and they were willing to work very hard. I basically came in and joined SAIC to help bring on the next generation of semi-automated forces.

Today, the Advanced Solutions team is intricately involved in modeling and simulation-based soldier training systems. In 2002, Leidos developed the U.S. Army's OneSAF program, a simulation platform that can solve existing as well as future problems that could arise on the battlefield. The system's open-source software can be reprogrammed to create new simulations that mirror real-life challenges that occur in theater. Among its many capabilities, OneSAF can evaluate a soldier's equipment while on patrol, command staff training, and even help identify domestic settings that are vulnerable to attack.

As a complement to the OneSAF program, in 2017 the U.S. Army Program Executive Office awarded Leidos a contract to help develop its Synthetic Environment Core (SE Core) Common Virtual Environment Management (CVEM) program. SE Core is a correlated terrain database that gives operators the ability to integrate live and virtual training simulations. Under the contract, Leidos is developing terrain data and battlefield equipment simulations to help train Army personnel under a variety of conditions. According to the company, the objective of SE Core is to enable interoperability within live, virtual, constructive, and gaming training systems to allow warfighters to train as they fight. "With SE Core, we are building the synthetic environmental representation of the world around us," said Shiflett. "The goal is to build the terrain of the entire world. There's about 147 million square kilometers of land surface on the earth, and I believe SE Core has recreated up to about 14.3 million square kilometers."

The Common Driver Trainer (CDT) system was designed to simulate dangerous real-life situations to train military drivers and crew.

In addition to OneSAF and SE Core, the Advanced Solutions team is also responsible for the development of the Common Driver Trainer (CDT) system. Since 2004, the company has been awarded six CDT contracts from the U.S. Army. The most recent award was in 2016.

The simulators provide training in critical tasks that would be too dangerous for drivers to simulate in real life. The system includes student training stations, after-action review, assistant driver stations, and four operator stations. While the simulation motions platforms are all the same, the simulator cabs are interchangeable, allowing users to train on a variety of vehicles, which is one of the features that sets these simulators apart from others. Training on the simulators can assist the crews of vehicles that include Mine Resistant Ambush Protected (MRAP) vehicles, M1A1 and M1A2 tanks, and the Joint Assault Bridge (JAB). Completed at a Leidos facility in Orlando, the system is destined for the driver-training program at Fort Leonard Wood.

When it comes to Leidos' work in simulation training, Shiflett said:

With OneSAF, you use a computer algorithm to drive a single tank or a collection of tanks. The terrain databases come from the SE Core program, which builds the environmental representation, and then we also build virtual simulators. We're trying to position Leidos to being on the leading edge of that technology and applying that technology to our customer's problem space, which is simulation and training.

Command and Control Solutions: Leidos Enterprise Architecture Framework (LEAF)

More than a decade ago, original equipment manufacturers (OEM) were, for the most part, the only players in the Department of Defense (DoD) Command and Control (C2) software realm, offering single monolithic solutions tightly tied to a vendor's products and codebase. Today, Leidos software Centers of Excellence develop highly complex C2 applications for the DoD quickly at low cost using industry leading Agile/DevOps practices. Teams have extensive experience modernizing legacy OEM applications into the most modern cloud-based, micro service-enabled architectures. These mission-critical systems are delivered using continuous integration/ continuous delivery pipelines, and deployed to customers' preferred environments, from "on-premise" to full cloud deployment. But how did Leidos crack the code?

In 2008, the Leidos team supported the U.S. Air Force Global War on Terror by defining and proving new integrated concepts of operation and delivering new software technology solutions into parts of the broader USAF C2 community. It became clear that the future of C2 lay in leveraging emerging framework-based software solutions that enabled distributed enterprise platforms that could deliver many smaller, highly tailorable applications adaptable to continually changing warfighter needs.

Leidos provides intricate modeling and simulation training for command conditions.

In 2011, Leidos began to leverage innovations in the software industry such as emerging commercial middleware components, Service Oriented Architecture (SOA) and open standards. This aligned its C2 system solution offering with commercial software approaches desired by the DoD and enabled development of solutions tailored to specific operational needs—something the commercial software vendors could not accomplish. Leidos was soon selected to develop the first modernized solution for the USAF Air Operations Center (AOC) modernization program.

At the same time, the R&D team recognized significant similarities in C2 systems across different operational domains and, using internal R&D funds, developed discriminating technologies that evolved into the Leidos Enterprise Application Framework (LEAF). This has enabled Leidos to modernize legacy C2 systems in a fraction of the time and cost of the traditional OEMs and deliver operationally relevant and deployable minimum viable products in just 3–4 months.

Leidos continues to invest and build on this success. Enabled by its commitment to framework-based platform solutions, the company has established two software factories recognized as Agile Centers of Excellence—modeled after Silicon Valley's Agile processes and DevOps methodologies—that combine reusable tools like LEAF with a matrixed staff trained and experienced in a broad set of technologies and domains. This formula has helped Leidos win and successfully execute more than $300 million of DoD and commercial programs over a large and diverse set of new business growth areas. The company has won multiple contract awards in the DoD C2 sector to modernize legacy applications for the USAF, U.S. Strategic Command and the U.S. Army. These awards included take-away wins that unseated incumbent OEMs, delivered complex, highly tailorable, mission-critical solutions on time and within budget, and

LEAF was extended into the Leidos health business as the technology baseline for the careC2 Pathways application, providing a single, consolidated environment for managing episodes of care with a common view for all care providers—including patient, family, case managers, and clinicians.

further cemented the Leidos C2 capabilities across the DoD. The solution was then extended into the Leidos health business, employing LEAF as the technology baseline for the careC2 Pathways product that enables large commercial healthcare systems to monitor, manage, and reduce deviations in patient care. LEAF also served as a key discriminator in the civil area's DHS Secure Enterprise Network Systems, Services & Support Contract (SENS3) win, a "$684 million award that represents not just one of the largest awards within DHS, but also a strategic opportunity for growth" in the company.

The continued growth and success of advanced solutions at Leidos is fueled by its core tenets of always putting the end-user first and building

Leidos CEO Roger Krone (left) with the winner for Excellence In Science and Technology, Research and Development, John Lawrence, (center, left) and Michael Raker (center right) accepting for the Rapid Legacy Modernization/ Distributed Command and Control Framework (RLSM/DC2F) Team, with then-National Security Sector President John Framatico Jr., (right) during the 2014 Leidos Achievement Awards ceremony on October 8, 2014.

adaptive solutions. As John Lawrence, a technology leader from the team's inception and now chief technology officer for the health business, said:

> *It is critical for us to deliver solutions that enable the customer to execute their mission exactly as they need, not forcing them to adapt their operations to our solution, even in the most minor areas. When their operations change, our solution must change as well.*

Through its platform strategy, the company's advanced solutions continually keep pace with advancing technology while avoiding vendor lock-in. Today, Leidos continues investing to meet the evolving needs of its customers, such as multi-domain C2 and the proliferation of autonomous systems, as well as leveraging advancing technologies such as cloud computing, AI/ML, micro-service designs, and DevOps practices. Vice President and Tech Fellow Mike Raker shared his insights on how Leidos maintains its success in the C2 sector moving forward:

> *Continuous innovation is hard to achieve, and requires multiple factors for success. It starts with leadership's continuous commitment to innovation and sets the tone for empowering all to dedicate himself or herself to the mission. Through these commitments, Leidos has bred a culture of innovation in our C2 market and SW factories far greater than the sum of those individuals comprising the teams. That culture is built to endure and continually meet our nation's toughest challenges. We rarely know how the next chapter will unfold, but when armed with committed leadership, and an empowered team with an innovative culture, Leidos will continually deliver the next innovation solution to our customers.*

The success of Leidos in advanced solutions can be attributed to its employees' free-thinking, team-oriented, and project-specific approach, a long-time staple of the Leidos culture since its days as SAIC.

Extended Reach

The Leidos entrepreneurial culture is often credited as the force behind the creative advanced solutions the company develops, which expand all across the company. "What we're looking to do is to determine how our technology can serve as a discriminator to support our work in health, civil, defense, and intelligence markets," said Chagnon.

Retired U.S. Air Force General John Jumper, former board member and former chairman and CEO of Leidos, attributes the company's success in Advanced Solutions to its freethinking and project-specific approach:

> We are going to make it without sort of proprietary jealousy about one kit or another that's going to solve our customer's problem. Developing the Sea Hunter *vessel, for instance, remains an example of the company developing something in-house that was tailored for the customer, instead of going to a subcontractor to develop the program. Those are the kinds of things that we do that remain the secret sauce that Bob Beyster would be proud of. This is the carryover from SAIC, and this is what I tell the employees, even today when I have a chance to stand up in front of them, and I just say, "Stand back. In the*

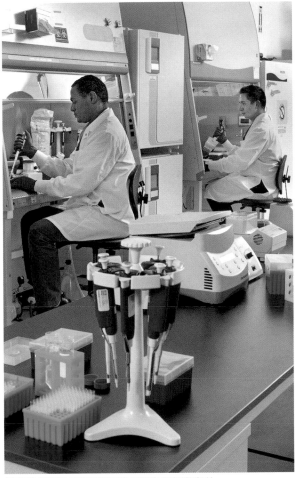

CREDIT: PHOTO COURTESY OF JAMES ARONOVSKY.

CREDIT: U.S. NAVY PHOTO BY JOHN F. WILLIAMS/RELEASED.*

hustle and bustle of your everyday work, it's difficult to stand back and admire what you've accomplished, and just to stand back and take a look at what you do for the nation, for the world, for your communities, for yourselves, is a very satisfying thing to do."

Chagnon also credits the free-thinking culture of entrepreneurship that J. Robert Beyster encouraged and nurtured, as well as the fostering of cross-collaboration, with allowing the company as a whole to thrive. He also believes much of the company's success is the result of the many unique and highly diverse fields of work Leidos is able to offer those who are up to the challenge, as he described:

Leidos offers countless opportunities for engineers and scientists of all disciplines to design and develop novel and innovative systems and technologies that will operate from the sea floor to outer space. You could be building a ship, designing sensors, integrating payloads on an aircraft, developing satellite payloads, creating training simulators, or writing the operational software that the Army uses for fire control management. The scope of opportunity in pretty much every region of this company is unlimited. ■

This page: The research and development work conducted in the area of advanced solutions supports health (left), civil (top right), and defense & intelligence (bottom right) applications.

*The appearance of U.S. Department of Defense (DoD) visual information does not imply or constitute DoD endorsement.

CHAPTER SEVEN

THE RIGHT PEOPLE IN THE RIGHT ROLES

We really wanted to make a difference to the nation as a company and as individuals.

_____

J. Robert Beyster, PhD
COMPANY FOUNDER

I N THE COMPANY'S EARLY DAYS, FOUNDER J. ROBERT BEYSTER WAS often asked for his "secret sauce" that allowed him to turn a small firm into a diversified, multinational corporation. Some would suggest it was the company's entrepreneurial culture, while others believed it was employee ownership. Beyster, however, always had the same answer: the people. "It is creating an environment that allows individuals to make a difference and be recognized for it," he wrote.

Patrick Bannister, who started with SAIC in 1975 and rose to the position of senior vice president, described the company's culture as "entrepreneurial and growth-oriented." Bannister came to the company after working for the EPA and supported some of the company's highest-profile projects, including a study on Agent Orange for the U.S. Air Force. Bannister explained that Beyster had a knack for bringing in the right people, "best of the breed, you know, really smart, willing to work incredibly hard, and willing to take some risks."

To find those right people, Beyster would look for an individual he considered a "triple threat." He defined that as an employee who could market and sell the solution, was a leading technical expert in his or her field, and could manage the work and those who performed it. "We really wanted to make a difference to the nation as a company and as individuals," Beyster wrote. "The best way we could do that was by solving challenging

Opposite: J. Robert Beyster would often say that employees were the "secret sauce" to the success of the company.

Then-SAIC's Public Safety Integration Center (PSIC)—a working laboratory that brought together more than 30 technology vendors, where federal officials could see how integrated systems work together.

technical problems that others might not or could not tackle. This was not rhetoric, and this strong desire helped us get some excellent people into the company who would make a difference."

That philosophy is still in place today. With the strength of the company's employees behind it, Leidos is able to deliver high-level systems throughout the world while retaining exceptional talent. The company has been widely lauded for its employee-centric culture, garnering numerous awards for being among the best places to work. Leidos now has 31,000 employees in more than 30 countries, and it continues to put, as Beyster explained, "people first."

1969

J. Robert Beyster's hand-written organizational plan—written shortly after founding SAI—calls for employee ownership as a hallmark of the company.

1987

Beyster creates a pamphlet called "The Principles and Practices of SAIC." It outlines 12 principles used to guide the company.

1999

SAIC, the country's largest employee-owned research and engineering firm, celebrates its 30th anniversary.

2003

After 34 years as the CEO of SAIC, founder J. Robert Beyster retires from the company.

Leidos Chairman and CEO Roger Krone said the culture Beyster created in the early days was something novel for any industry. "What Bob was able to do with an absolute clean sheet of paper from day one, creating involvement and engagement of all employees in a way that no other company has ever been able to do, allowed all employees to become owners from day one."

That culture remains today, as Krone follows the core values of the company's previous CEOs in adopting Beyster's management style:

> *When I took the job, part of what they don't tell you is how deep the employee empowerment, employee ownership culture is at this company. So I'm not the boss at the top of the organizational structure. I'm at the bottom of the organizational structure. I have 31,000 bosses, and an open e-mail account.*

Today, Leidos Chairman and CEO Roger Krone has maintained Beyster's culture while incorporating his own vision into Leidos.

People First

From its earliest days, SAI recognized and celebrated diverse ideas and ways of thinking. "The company's greatest strength is that while there is a common bond that holds these people together, there is no evidence that everyone thinks alike," biographer Stan Burns wrote in *SAIC: The First Thirty Years*. "History shows that controlled chaos inside the walls of SAIC has gotten the company to where it is today: well-placed on a sturdy foundation and ready to move forward on a number of different fronts."

2003

SAIC is awarded the Frost & Sullivan Defense and Aerospace Division Market Leadership award in Homeland Security and Homeland Defense.

2009

SAIC celebrates its 40th anniversary, evolving from a small business in La Jolla, California, to an international company.

2009

Ken Dahlberg, who succeeded Beyster as CEO and chairman of the board of directors, retires. Former BAE Systems, Inc. CEO Walt Havenstein takes over as CEO of SAIC.

2012

John Jumper, a retired U.S. Air Force general, assumes the CEO position during the transition from SAIC to Leidos.

Retired U.S. Air Force Major General Robert "Rosie" Rosenberg served as an executive vice president for SAIC. *(Photo by Christian Ramirez.)*

Robert "Rosie" Rosenberg, a retired U.S. Air Force major general who later worked as an executive vice president for SAIC, said he found two things impressive about Beyster. First was the fact that he had tossed away millions of dollars by giving his company to his employees. "That wasn't the senior line managers," Rosenberg said. "It was scientists, engineers, marketers, contracts people, secretaries, personnel—anybody who was helping the growth of the company." Second was that Beyster was always willing to serve on government committees and boards and encouraged his employees to do the same:

[Beyster's] attitude toward the growth of the company wasn't to make money for him; it was to serve our country. And it was either serve the country through our systems engineering, systems integration, software

2014

Roger Krone (right) succeeds General John Jumper (left) as CEO of Leidos. He works to ensure the company is aligned to support the customer's mission following the spin-off of the new SAIC.

2015

Business Insider ranks Leidos as the 42nd best place to work in America, in part due to the company's generous wages and benefits.

2016

JANUARY

The merger of Leidos and Lockheed Martin's IS&GS business is announced.

2016

The *Washington Business Journal* recognizes Leidos for Deal of the Year during its annual Best in Business Awards.

development, or through the only hardware business we were in, which was
nuclear because of his own background in that.

Beyster's modus operandi was implemented at the start of then-SAI.
He knew that most companies avoided risks associated with underperforming
staff by curtailing freedoms and setting rules for daily operations. The company
handbook, *Principles and Practices of SAIC*, envisioned another way, defining
the company as one with a "free and open company environment" that allowed
for constructive criticism in search of "better ways to run our business."

To avoid exposure to financial risk resulting from
such autonomy, Beyster developed "very tight fiscal
controls." This created a near scientific scrutiny of
ideas to ensure they had merit and were in the best
interest of customers, as well as scrutiny of financial
goals and organizational decisions.

Mary Ann Beyster, daughter of the company
founder, said her father's philosophy continued at
home, where he encouraged his children to be
curious and seek understanding of why and how
things were happening. With this approach,
Beyster expected his employees to take ownership.
"I wouldn't disagree that the company was often
referred to as Bob Beyster's company. That said, he
would take offense to that because it was an
employee-owned company," Mary Ann Beyster said.
"He expected and wanted to inspire people to act
like it was their own company, and, in fact, that's
exactly what they did."

An important part
of Beyster's vision
was to inspire
employees to act
like SAI was their
own company.

2017

Leidos returns to
the FORTUNE 500®
list at number 381.

2017

The Human Rights
Campaign names
Leidos as one of its
Best Places to
Work, with a
100 percent score
on its annual
Corporate Equality
Index.

2017

Leidos is ranked
number 18 on
Defense News'
Top 100 list. The
company also
makes the list for
Forbes' Best
Management
Consulting Firms,
coming in at
number 447.

2018

Ethisphere®
Institute names
Leidos one of the
World's Most
Ethical Companies.

CONTINUING A LEGACY

In 2003, company founder J. Robert Beyster retired after 34 years at the helm of SAIC. Leidos, now at its 50th anniversary, has been led by just four more CEOs, who have contributed their own ideas and vision to the company.

Ken Dahlberg succeeded Beyster as CEO and chairman of the board of directors and remained in that role until his retirement in 2009. Walt Havenstein, former CEO of BAE North America, then took over the CEO position. Retired U.S. Air Force General John Jumper was named CEO in 2012, shortly before the transition from SAIC to Leidos. Roger Krone took over as CEO of Leidos in 2014.

"If you want the business to continue as successfully as its potential would suggest, then you need somebody like Roger Krone, and here we had this opportunity to get this guy who was extraordinarily successful," Jumper said. "I put my hat on then as a board member and said, 'This is the right thing to do.'" After becoming CEO, Krone said he knew he had to "mend some of the wounds" from the split with what is now the new SAIC and return the company to the main focus of being in alignment with the customer's mission. Krone said, "From that point on, it's been a pretty exciting and rewarding journey. We've now doubled the size of the company, and we're performing really well in our programs. I think we've made it a great place for people to come to work. We're building the Leidos brand, and we're building it through performance."

Leidos' efforts to put employees first and give them opportunities have landed the company on multiple lists of the best places to work. In 2015, *Business Insider* ranked Leidos 42nd on its list of the best companies to work for in America. The publication lauded the company for its generous wages: after five years, the median employee salary was $85,600. Leidos also boasted a 70 percent job satisfaction rating, in part due to a myriad of benefits, which include carpooling services, low-cost bus passes, and telecommuting opportunities.

Ray Veldman, senior vice president, deputy general counsel, and corporate secretary, who joined the company in 2008, said of Leidos:

> *What I enjoy most about working at Leidos is working with my colleagues in the legal department and elsewhere throughout the organization. With the collegiality that we have here and the smart people that we employ, it's really a joy to come to work. People are the most important part of the job.*

Retired Marine Corps Major General Arnold Punaro, former SAIC executive vice president and general manager for Leidos Washington operations, explained that those who come to work at Leidos help ensure the safety of all American citizens:

> *You want to work on something that's going to make the United States of America safer for your kids and your grandkids and your great-grandkids. You want to work at Leidos because that's the kind of work they do each and every day.*

Technical Expertise

Leidos staff members are highly specialized in a diverse set of technical skills. Among the company's 31,000 employees, nearly 40 percent have earned degrees in science, technology, engineering, and mathematics (STEM) fields of study. Those with master's degrees total 6,300, and nearly 1,000 employees possess PhDs. Some 93 percent of Leidos' staff is in the United States, while 7 percent work internationally.

One of the company's thought leaders is Dr. John J. Fratamico Jr., chief technology officer for Leidos. Fratamico said he first cultivated an interest in electromagnetics from an MIT professor. At Leidos, he discovered a company whose employees expressed the same type of excitement for the sciences. "Leidos employees are some of the best and brightest in this industry and offer expertise across a broad portfolio of technical solutions," Fratamico said.

Under Dr. John J. Fratamico Jr.'s (above) leadership, Leidos led the team that designed and built DARPA's Anti-Submarine Warfare (ASW) Continuous Trail Unmanned Vessel (below) now named *Sea Hunter*. The vessel is capable of operating over thousands of kilometers on the open sea for months at a time.

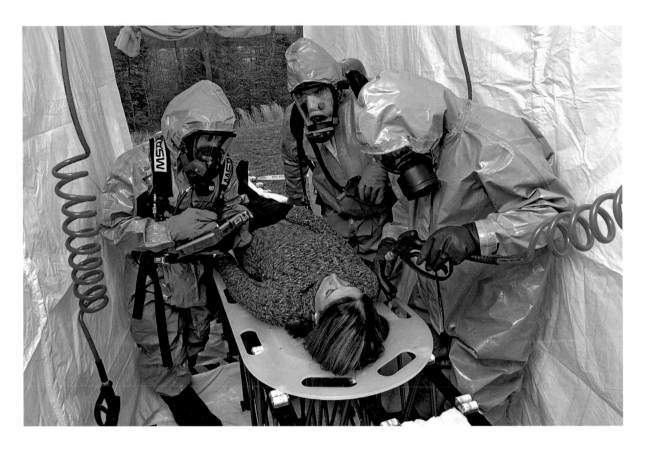

The Guardian Installation Protection Program is comprised of several systems that supplement other aspects of force protection against potential weapons of mass destruction. Leidos employees are drawn to the company for the opportunity to do important work that makes a difference in people's lives around the world.

Part of the company's efforts to attract highly educated employees includes partnering with top universities. In November 2017, Leidos Australia partnered with the University of New South Wales to cooperate on research and development of biological security protections for the Australian Defence Force. Under the agreement, Leidos will help improve detection and response to threats that include biological, chemical, and radiological weapons that target Australia. The company and university will also assist hazmat teams in responding more effectively to potential attacks from hazardous materials.

Leidos has been successful at attracting highly educated and experienced employees by offering employees the chance to do something meaningful, according to Melissa Koskovich, senior vice president, director of communications and marketing. Koskovich leads a team of professionals who are responsible for "the voice" of the company, including internal and executive communications, marketing, advertising, creative and branding, media relations, corporate social responsibility, and community outreach. Formerly with U.S. Air Force public affairs, Koskovich, who came to the company in 1998, said of its mission:

Come to Leidos if you want to do work that is important, work that makes a difference. We don't sell socks. Our CEO will say that from time to time. We don't make a new and improved toothpaste, right? We're going to help cure

cancer. We're going to help defend our nation. We're going to improve your
experience at an airport when you travel with your family. We're going to make
it safe, and we're going to make it easier. That's the sort of work that we do here.
If you want your life's work to matter, come to Leidos.

Establishing Longevity

A vast majority of employees stay at Leidos for a significant portion of their professional career. Two-thirds of employees have been with the company at least three years, and 19 percent of all employees have remained there for 15 years or more.

Jim Russell was employee number 110 when he came to work for the company in 1972 and remains as a consultant. When he started, SAIC's gross revenue was at $2 million, and it grew quickly to $11 million in that next year. In 1988, Russell landed the company's first billion-dollar contract, for the Composite Health Care System (CHCS).

He said he remained with the company so long because of the culture Beyster built, one where hard work was both expected and appreciated. "[Beyster] used to call me at 9 o'clock in the morning here, 6 o'clock his time, to talk, so he was up working at six in the morning," Russell recalled. "When I set up the proposal center, he called me the second week, and that's when he said, 'Hey, I drove by the proposal center last night at 9 o'clock, and the lights weren't on. What's going on?'"

Beyster's commitment to the company and the culture of employee ownership he created were critical factors in the decision for valuable thought leaders like Russell to stay with the organization for several years.

From left to right: Leidos Chairman and CEO Roger Krone presents the 2015 Achievement Award for Excellence in Program Management for Large Programs to the Armed Forces Health Longitudinal Technology Application (AHLTA)/ Composite Heath Care System (CHCS) Team represented by Pat McGrath, Karla Klussendorf, and then-Executive Vice President and Health Sector President Jon Scholl.

The International Space Station (ISS), as seen from the space shuttle *Atlantis* in 2011. Leidos is currently working on a project with the ISS and expects the company's role with NASA to expand in the future. Since 2011, Leidos has packed and processed 135,000 lbs. of supplies for the International Space Station, traveling more than 950,000 miles. *(Photo courtesy of NASA.)*

Leidos has achieved its ability to retain talent in part through diversity programs that have earned the company industry accolades. In 2017, the Corporate Equality Index—a national benchmarking survey and report on workplace conditions—awarded Leidos a perfect score in recognition of the company's policies and practices related to lesbian, gay, bisexual, transgender, and queer (LGBTQ) workplace equality. Among the company's efforts is the PRIDE Employee Resource Group (ERG), which connects employees in an effort to foster understanding of LGBTQ issues. Former Leidos Chief Human Resources Officer Ann Addison said:

> *Leidos encourages and celebrates a culture of innovation and high performance through diversity of thought, which is only achieved by embracing all perspectives within our employee population.*

Gloria Spikes is a 44-year veteran employee based in Houston, Texas. She is currently working on a project with the International Space Station and sees Leidos expanding its role with NASA in the future to work on deep-space missions. Spikes believes employees remain at Leidos due to the ample opportunities to work on such exciting projects. "In the Leidos environment, you can move around. You can come here with one major, but you can see other associated majors and things that you can go into," Spikes said. "It gives you chances to seem like you've been in college forever. You get a chance to learn new things, and you can move around, so it's a forever-learning environment."

OPERATION MVP

Leidos has a long-standing track record of hiring veterans and giving priority to attracting new talent from the military. Approximately 6,500 employees, or one in five of the workforce, are veterans of the U.S. Armed Forces.

From 2014 to 2017 alone, the company hired more than 4,900 veterans. The Leidos Operation MVP (Military Veteran Program) furthers the aim of helping and recruiting veterans. The program teams Leidos with veterans' organizations and military transition centers to identify potential recruits and assist them with career development. Along with the Department of Labor and Center for a New American Security initiatives, Leidos also works with wounded warriors to offer employment search training. The efforts have earned Leidos awards, including *U.S. Veteran's Magazine* Best of the Best Top Veteran-Friendly Companies and Victory Media's Top 100 Military Friendly Employers and Military Spouse Friendly Employers.

In May 2016, the company took part in a ceremony at the White House to announce new private sector hiring and training for veterans and their spouses. At Leidos, veterans are paired up with an onboarding representative to help them during the first 90 days, and can assimilate with other veterans in the company's Military Alliance Group (MAG). The Operation MVP program has been such a success that Leidos has an ambitious but promising goal of hiring another 3,000 veterans by 2021. Dale Crewe, president of MAG, commented, "One of the most stressful and important decisions when transitioning out of the military is making your next career move. After 12-plus years with Leidos, I have no regrets with my decision."

Above: Michele Brown admired then-SAIC's culture and its people so much while she worked as the company's legal counsel at an outside firm that she decided to join the company in 2008. Today she is a senior vice president and the chief ethics and compliance officer.

Right: Leidos is the largest employer of private-sector employees contracted to work for U.S. surveillance agencies. Pictured here is a Leidos employee working at a Command and Control/ Operations Center.

Leidos Chief Ethics and Compliance Officer Michele Brown was in private practice for the law firm Holland & Knight in 2000 when she took on SAIC as a client. "I became so impressed then by the company's culture, by its brand, and most of all, its people," she said. Brown admired the employees' education and knowledge, dedication to the mission, and drive to solve some of the most complex and challenging problems a company and its customers in this industry could face. Brown was so enamored she decided to join the company in 2008 and is now the chief ethics and compliance officer. Brown added, "It's just an extraordinary place to work, and after I came on board in 2008, that respect and admiration only deepened when I had the opportunity to really work side by side with these individuals."

National Security

Leidos Senior Vice President and Chief Security Officer Charlie Price reported that 12,000 Leidos employees (nearly 40 percent of the company's workforce) had security clearances, with 68 percent of those security clearances at Top Secret level and higher.

A comprehensive study on public and private employment in intelligence conducted by Tim Shorrock of *The Nation* found Leidos to be the largest employer of private-sector employees contracted to work for U.S. surveillance agencies.

Left: Leidos provides training and analytical services to the U.S. Department of Defense and Intelligence Community facilities supporting U.S. and coalition forces during their critical missions.

Below: Before serving as the 23rd Secretary of the United States Air Force, Deborah Lee James led SAIC's Technology and Engineering Sector. *(Photo courtesy of U.S. Air Force by Jim Varhegyi.)**

Leidos offers a multitude of services to the Intelligence Community, serving in some capacity for most of the 17 organizations that comprise the community. The Department of Homeland Security (DHS) hired the company in 2017 to modernize its Homeland Secure Data Network and its Classified Local Area Network. The five-year, $684 million contract will assure Homeland Security data can be shared safely with intelligence and law enforcement communities. Leidos not only operates the network, but also assures its security, optimization, and ongoing enhancement to adjust to changes in the intelligence sector. "We're proud that DHS has entrusted Leidos to operate and modernize its enterprise systems to support information sharing and intelligence missions across all DHS components, including federal, state, local, and tribal partners," said Angela Heise, president of the company's civil business. "Our operational excellence and understanding of DHS mission-critical needs will streamline information sharing across all DHS stakeholders."

Before serving as the 23rd Secretary of the United States Air Force, Deborah Lee James led SAIC's Technology and Engineering Sector. "Employees work on the premise that they will be asked to solve some of the most difficult challenges the country faces," said James when asked about the company's culture. "So whether it is working on national security issues, whether it is working on health issues, you will be tackling some of those tough problems and providing solutions. I would say another thing is you'll be in with really smart people—great people." ■

CHAPTER EIGHT

CUSTOMER FIRST

When I was with the Seventh Air Force in Korea before I retired, SAIC helped me with a significant problem by bringing science to solutions. It was that mind-set of understanding the customer, fact-based presentation and recommendations, and an understanding of science—in this case, the North Korea threat, particularly the chemical launch ballistic missiles—that impressed me so much about the company. And then, happily, I ended up consulting for them.

Charles Heflebower
LIEUTENANT GENERAL, USAF (RETIRED)
FORMER LEIDOS EMPLOYEE

C USTOMERS ARE AN ESSENTIAL PART OF LEIDOS' SUCCESS, and the company's dedication to its clients is the number-one goal. Leidos' ability to forge these generation-long relationships is rooted in the company's founding, when J. Robert Beyster committed to creating synergistic partnerships with customers. Those partnerships have literally taken Leidos to the ends of the Earth and beyond—from Antarctica and the greatest depths of the sea to outer space.

Beyster had a specific vision for how the company would seek to become profitable. Unlike other enterprises that sought to extract the largest profits out of ventures, Beyster decided the company would never seek to "make a quick buck at the expense of its mostly government customers." Instead, he saw customers as collaborators working to reach the same goals. "Our philosophy of making a reasonable profit permeated the organization," Beyster wrote. "Employees were able to deal with customers more comfortably because there was no pressure to generate high profits."

That theory produced the type of long-term relationships Beyster hoped to generate. Between Leidos and its recently acquired IS&GS business, the company has relationships that span decades. Leidos has relationships with at least 10 companies and government agencies that span 10 years, eight that span 20 years, five that span 30 years, and five lasting more than 40 years.

Opposite: Leidos' varied customers each have specific needs and requirements the company is well suited to handle.

Betty Bidwell began working for the company in 1974 as a temporary typist and now works in international trade compliance. Bidwell said Beyster created a culture where Leidos employees are expected to listen to the customer to understand what they truly need. "It was an exciting, dynamic culture," Bidwell said. "It was a lot of work that was critical to the country. It was a culture and an environment of: roll up your sleeves, dig in, help out wherever you can, help other programs, help other people, working with the client, making sure that we were meeting the client's needs. And the philosophy was: be where the client is, and that's really what we did. We developed relationships with our clients to make sure that we understood them."

A New Way of Forging Contracts

In its first two decades, SAIC had a multitude of key discriminators to win new business. Often, it was the only company with the technological know-how and advanced equipment to compete. However, in the 1980s, two major changes forced the company to rethink the way it bid and won contracts. First, more companies developed the technological skills to be competitive on large government and private-sector contracts. Second, the federal government began requiring companies to submit fixed-price bids that made the process far more difficult and competitive. By 1985, SAIC had revised and improved its process of submitting bids in part by expanding marketing efforts, assuring that the company could continue to be a leader in this new era.

The company's new approach to bids meant more partnerships with outside companies and firms. Among them, SAIC partnered in 1986 with

1969

J. Robert Beyster establishes founding philosophies for his new company, "that SAI will listen to its customers first and consider any contract, no matter its size."

1969

The U.S. government becomes the company's first customer, hiring Beyster's firm to analyze nuclear weapon effects. "After a year, a surprising thing happened," Beyster said. "We made a profit."

1985

SAIC
An Employee-Owned Company

The company rethinks its limited marketing approach to contracts so it can remain competitive in a new era where smaller companies offer competitive technologies.

1986

SAIC and California Microwave team up to create an unmanned aerial vehicle that would become a precursor to future drone aircraft.

California Microwave's Government Electronics Division to develop
Intelligence Electronic Warfare/Unmanned Aerial Vehicles (IEW/UAV).
The vehicles then competed for a U.S. Army contract to develop them
for use in the field. While it was unknown then, SAIC's work on this project
would help pave the way for the drones that have become ubiquitous in
wartime and intelligence-gathering operations today.

Kim D. Denver is Leidos' senior vice president and chief corporate
contracts executive. After Denver joined the company in 2013, he oversaw the initiative to combine contracts with procurement into a single
organization. This new approach allowed those working on contracts
to "negotiate with the buy side and the sell side in mind," as he stated,
so that those trying to win contracts could work in concert with those
working with suppliers.

Then-SAIC's work
on Intelligence
Electronic Warfare/
Unmanned Aerial
Vehicles for the
U.S. Army in the
late 1980s helped
pave the way for
modern drones
such as the MQ-1
Predator (left)
and its successor,
the MQ-9 Reaper.
*(U.S. Air Force photo/
Staff Sgt. Vernon
Young Jr.)**

1987

The rugged laptop
the company
develops for the
U.S. Army, called
a Lightweight
Computer Unit
(LCU), becomes
ubiquitous in
field computing
and popular
among
government
agencies and
private-sector
companies.

1991

CREDIT: PHOTO COURTESY OF NASA.

After years of
smaller contracts
mostly with field
centers, NASA
awards the
company its first
major contract,
$150 million over a
decade, develop-
ing satellites to
gather information
about the Earth.

1992

British Petroleum
hires SAIC to
handle $20 million
of its IT work in
Alaska, Great
Britain, and South
America. The
contract soon
expands and
solidifies the
company as a
major player in IT
and in the oil and
gas industry.

1992

IMAGE CREDIT: VECTEEZY.COM

SAIC's workforce
blossoms to
14,500 employees,
including
international
locations.

Denver said of the company's work with its customers and suppliers:

> *At the end of the day, our work is about collectively working very closely with our customers and suppliers, developing those relationships, techniques, and tools so that we can shape requirements either on the customer side or shape strategies on the sell side to support the needs as we go to market with our supplies and services for the government.*

Going the Extra Mile

Leidos has worked for more than 40 years with five U.S. government agencies—the Army, the Navy, the Department of Defense, the Federal Aviation Administration, and NASA—developing vital solutions that have kept Americans safe in the air, on the ground, on the water, and in outer space. Much of the company's early success with these agencies was a result of Beyster's insistence on making sure that his customers were completely satisfied with the finished product. Retired U.S. Air Force General Robert "Rosie" Rosenberg knows this firsthand. While working in strategic planning for the Air Force, Rosenberg was in charge of a nuclear exchange software program being developed by SAIC. The colonel running the program asked Rosenberg for an additional half-million dollars to finish the project. But when the colonel came back and asked for more money the following year, Rosenberg decided to cancel the project.

Rosenberg recalled the phone call from Beyster:

> *Beyster called me on the phone and said, "Why are you terminating this contract?" And I said, "Because the guy that works for me lied to me.*

1997

Petróleos de Venezuela, S.A., the state-owned oil company of Venezuela, and SAIC create a 1,500-employee IT company, expanding the company's footprint in terms of the market sectors and international customers it serves.

2007

SAIC uses the $4.5 million Holland Computing Center supercomputer to help build simulators that train those in combat and first response. The University of Nebraska at Omaha supercomputer is among the world's fastest and can help predict types of attacks before they occur.

2015

Leidos works with NATS to introduce "Time-Based Separation" to Heathrow Airport. The system makes a 62 percent improvement to the airport's effectiveness during strong headwinds, saving 100,000 minutes of delays yearly.

2017

International customers account for 9 percent of Leidos' revenue.

He told me, when I gave him the money last year, that that was the end of it.
It was all taken care of, and you guys are sucking me dry." Beyster then said,
"Forget it. I'm finishing the program at no cost to you."

In 1988, when Rosenberg decided to enter the private sector, he took a job as SAIC's senior vice president in charge of strategic planning. Within a year, Beyster had promoted him to sector manager in charge of the military space business. Rosenberg said of Beyster: "The way he raised people in the company to care first about what they were doing for their customers was to me what made him such a famous person in our country's history."

Retired U.S. Navy Admiral Bobby Ray Inman had a similar experience with the company. After Inman retired from the Navy in 1982, he had multiple offers to join civilian firms, either as an employee or a director of the board. Inman entertained only one offer—Beyster's request to join the SAIC board, which he ultimately agreed to.

While doing his due diligence in researching SAIC, Inman heard a story from a retired submariner:

> *They had had a contract with SAIC. They were*
> *not pleased with the outcome, and because they*
> *were not pleased, Beyster agreed to totally redo it at*
> *his own cost and did, and they were very pleased*
> *with the outcome. So that told me the attitude about*
> *delivering quality.*

After considering several offers, retired Admiral Bobby Ray Inman accepted a seat on SAIC's board due to the reputation the company enjoyed with its customers. *(Official CIA Photo, courtesy of Wikimedia.)*

2017

Leidos and NATS become charter members of the International Standards Organization's (ISO) 44001 certification, which focuses on the improvement of collaboration between companies and their customers.

2017

The Leidos air traffic management system, Skyline, goes operational in South Korea. A large portion of the world's flights and the world's oceanic airspace is overseen by Leidos systems.

2017

NASA contracts with Leidos to pack pressurized cargo headed to the International Space Station through a $159 million contract.

2018

Leidos launches its Alliance Partner Network, a program designed to strengthen the connection with its suppliers and leverage their most advanced technologies to deliver customer mission success.

Customers with Worldwide Impact

In 2017, 9 percent of Leidos' $10.17 billion in revenue came from international customers. During the 1980s and 1990s, the company saw rapid growth internationally, and by 1992, its workforce had grown to 14,500 employees in offices throughout the globe. International contracts ranged from a workstation scoring system for the 1992 Summer Olympics in Barcelona to the world's first fuel-cell-powered transit bus for Ballard Power Systems of Canada.

One of the more visible international projects Leidos has supported is for the United Kingdom's Ministry of Defence (MoD) in the development

LEIDOS IS THE CUSTOMER

Leidos not only has vital relationships with its own customers, but the company *is the* customer when dealing with its more than 17,000 suppliers. "Roughly 40 percent of all Leidos programs are dependent upon companies outside of Leidos," said Bob Gemmill, vice president of strategic sourcing, who added:

What my team has done in conjunction with our CTO, is we said, "You know what? If we don't have a strategy for that 40 percent of the business, we're really not putting our best foot forward with our customer, and we're not going to be competitive." So we've put some new things in place to better extract the value out of that 40 percent of the business that's outsourced to our suppliers, and we've done that through a formal supplier relationship

management program. So if you're a large or a critical supplier to Leidos, you have an executive assigned who owns that relationship at that level, and in some cases, that executive is Roger Krone, our CEO.

In 2018, Leidos established the Leidos Alliance Partner Network, which strengthens connections and encourages collaboration with suppliers in the effort to drive innovation, advance technology, and build efficiency that ultimately benefits the customer. "The Leidos Alliance Partner Network is something we created because we wanted to develop better relationships with a very targeted set of our supplier partners," said Tony Leiter, director of strategic technology sourcing. Leiter continued:

We have very tight integration on the technical side, and the capture

of their Logistic Commodities & Services Transformation (LCST) program. The company's work on LCST serves to enhance the U.K.'s defense supply chain by providing efficient and cost-saving solutions for procurement, storage, inventory management, and distribution of materiel, including food, packed fuels, and clothing. Using near-real-time data monitoring, reporting, and analysis, LCST provides the MoD's front line commands with immediate access to the supplies they need when they need them.

Another Leidos international customer, NATS, has worked with the company's heritage IS&GS for more than 30 years. Formally known as the National Air Traffic Services, NATS is the leading provider of air traffic control services in the United Kingdom and a provider for such services

pipelines are shared from business development to the supplier, so we can team early and often, which allows us to get the right resources and the right experts from each of our technology suppliers engaged early in the proposal to give us a much better strategy going forward.

In addition to participating in management and collaboration initiatives, Leidos and its suppliers must adhere to Federal Acquisition Regulation (FAR) guidelines and oversee supplier compliance to address issues that include: security, hazmat identification, whistleblower protections, and other complex issues. The selection of suppliers is guided by the Leidos Code of Conduct, a document that guides each step, from supplier selection criteria to the execution of the contract. "The Code is a broad statement of principles that guides each of us toward doing the right thing," wrote Leidos CEO Roger Krone in the Code of Conduct's introduction.

In addition to large suppliers, Leidos also has a long history of being a customer to small businesses, including those owned by women and the disadvantaged. In 2016, Leidos awarded $922 million in contracts through its Small Business Program. Those efforts earned the company a "Highly Successful" rating from the Defense Contract Management Agency.

Furthermore, Leidos' award-winning mentor-protégé program demonstrates the company's commitment to small businesses that can provide both affordable and high-quality products and services. The company's Strategic Sourcing program is an ongoing effort to analyze third-party contracts and revalidate agreements to assure suppliers meet standards of price, quality, and performance. These efforts run in conjunction with Leidos' commitment to work with veteran-owned firms that can deliver high-quality products while also helping those who have served in the U.S. military transition to civilian life. Leidos' efforts to work with small businesses have earned the company 30 awards, including those from the Small Business Administration and NASA's Large Business Prime Contractor of the Year Award.

Leidos oversees a majority of the world's oceanic airspace for many international customers.

around the globe. NATS provides services to 14 airports, 250 million passengers, and 2.4 million flights yearly across multiple continents.

Since the founding of SAI, Beyster always encouraged employees to be innovative in how they worked with their customers, and collaboration was always at the forefront. In 2017, an official benchmark on collaboration between companies and clients was put in place with the creation of the International Standards Organization's (ISO) 44001 certification. Leidos and NATS were two of the first organizations to become certified. "For international work, the ISO is the standard setter," said Bill Krampf, current vice president and division manager and former senior vice president for Leidos U.K. and Europe, who worked with NATS for many years. "The important part for us on that is, Leidos and NATS are charter members of the ISO 44001 certification, which is focused on collaboration. So we're really leveraging that when we go talk to customers because collaboration has always been a central part of what we do, and that ISO certification shows our customers just how serious we are about it."

Today, Leidos continues working and collaborating with NATS to support their current systems and to help develop the next generation of air traffic control. Stuart Crawford, the U.K. air traffic management programs director at Leidos, described what he believes sets Leidos apart when it comes to serving its customers both domestically and overseas:

One of the reasons I've stayed with the company for so long is because of the commitment that our people show in making our customers successful. That may sound a bit glib, but, honestly, we see it day in and day out. It's easy to be supportive and work well when things are going good, but it's when there are a few bumps in the road that I think our employees absolutely come to the fore, and that's why we have such long-standing relationships with our customers, because we continually deliver and go the extra mile for them.

NO CONTRACT TOO SMALL

While Leidos has a long history with NASA, including multimillion-dollar contracts, many of the company's early assignments with the space agency were on small-dollar projects. From the outset, J. Robert Beyster believed that no contract was too small. As long as a new job could help cover an employee's salary while still forging a profit, it was acceptable.

"We believed in a value of small beginnings," Beyster wrote. "As our experience showed, small things often beget large things." The company discovered that it could forge new relationships through contracts that other companies might snub for being too small. This proved especially true with NASA.

That changed in 1989, when SAIC hired Neil Hutchinson. A former flight controller during the Apollo missions, Hutchinson had risen to flight director of Mission Control at the Johnson Space Center in Houston.

After Hutchinson left NASA, Beyster appointed him to direct SAIC's efforts with the space agency. Hutchinson decided to target the Mission to Planet Earth program, which was developing satellites to gather information about the Earth. In 1991, SAIC won a $150 million contract over 10 years, tripling the amount of work the company performed for the space agency.

Today, Leidos maintains multiple high-level contracts with NASA. Among them is a $159 million contract signed in 2017 to pack pressurized cargo for delivery to the International Space Station. That contract is handled by a Houston-based team, which supplies NASA with hardware and flight crew equipment to support deliveries to the space station.

The NASA contracts demonstrate that Beyster's theory of using small contracts as stepping-stones continues to be effective. "As our expansion into space programs showed," Beyster wrote, "this philosophy sometimes led to significant opportunities for the company."

Acquiring Competencies Solidifies Relationships

Leidos' technology solutions are not limited to government contracts. The company's work extends to the private sector as well. This type of work began in 1992 after Cheryl Louie, an operations research analyst for the company, moved into management. Louie had been working on a NASA space station software program in Houston, Texas, and once that contract was secured, she began looking at other possibilities in the area.

Louie learned that British Petroleum (BP) sought to outsource its IT operations, worth hundreds of millions of dollars a year. The company partnered with Sema Group and Syncordia to submit a bid. BP chose the company to handle $20 million of the work yearly. The contract covered operations in Alaska, Great Britain, and South America. Initially, the contract was responsible for the analysis of how BP could run its IT operations more efficiently, but it quickly grew to include more responsibilities. Beyster wrote, "The BP contract built SAIC's reputation as a first-rate competitor in the emerging field of IT outsourcing, acquiring competencies that could be— and were—successfully applied to capture customers in multiple industries and markets, to include oil and gas, utilities, and others."

Today, Leidos is one of the largest pure-play IT service providers to the U.S. government overseas. Anita K. Jones, who served on the board of directors twice between 1997 and 2014, said Leidos was able to branch into IT and various other areas of work because Beyster created a company that was highly decentralized. "We had many small offices in different parts

Employees working on servers at the Leidos data center in Gaithersburg, Maryland.

of the country, mainly because they were near our customers," said Jones. "And so the employee and the customer were co-located; that way, employees could be very responsive to their needs."

In terms of the customer-service-oriented culture Beyster created, Jones added:

> *Beyster would frequently say that we measure our success in terms of our customer's having success. That was always part of the culture of the company. And so I think that makes it a very attractive place to be. If you contribute, you're respected and incentivized to do more and to be given more authority, more responsibility.*

From the day Beyster founded the company, Leidos has continually raised the bar on finding high-level solutions with the goal of exceeding customers' expectations on both quality and price. Company employees have also been taught to go a step further when taking on a project by looking for opportunities where improvements can be made in areas their clients may not be aware of. "For us, setting ourselves apart means customer first, and it means understanding what the customer is going to need in the near future and helping them see through that, and in leaning in to develop those solutions more proactively," Leidos Chief Financial Officer James Reagan said. "These are the kinds of things that, in the future, with continuing constraints that our customers are going to see on budgets, we can help deliver more at the same level of spend." ■

CHAPTER NINE

GOING PUBLIC

We are here to start a new phase in our company's history.

——————

Kenneth Dahlberg
FORMER SAIC CHAIRMAN AND CEO

E MPLOYEE OWNERSHIP WAS LONG THE HALLMARK OF SAIC, as closely intertwined with the company's roots as the firm's commitment to using science to improve society. Therefore, it was a surprise to many when the company announced in 2005 that it would be launching an initial public offering (IPO), taking SAIC onto the stock market and trading as a public company.

In looking deeper at SAIC's decision to go public, it became clear that employees were still at the forefront of the company's decision. Not only did employee shareholders vote to approve the decision to take the company to the stock exchange, in fact, after going public, SAIC employees still held the vast majority of the voting power of the company's stock, which kept them in place as the firm's decision makers.

While the idea of going public had been discussed since the company's early days, founder J. Robert Beyster had dismissed it, fearing the stock market would not understand the complexities of SAIC. "Bob used to say, 'I'm just worried that we're such a complicated, complex company that the markets won't get us, because we work on all these national security programs, and you can't talk about them,'" recalled Ron Zollars, Beyster's former chief of staff who is now the programs and communications director at The Beyster Institute. Zollars added:

Opposite: A banner outside the New York Stock Exchange on October 13, 2006, declares "The Next Generation of SAIC is Here."

Frank Kendall, a member of the Leidos Board of Directors, believed in the employee ownership program instilled by Beyster, but as the company grew, many agreed the business model would no longer be sustainable.

The customers—they're covert programs, black programs. And so you know how analysts are: They want to dig in and learn about everything, and it's like: "Well, I'm sorry. We can't talk about this. We can't talk about that one, either." And [Beyster] just didn't feel that the markets would be as accepting.

Thankfully for Beyster and all of the employees at the company, the markets were accepting. On October 13, 2006, SAIC began trading on the New York Stock Exchange under the ticker symbol, SAI, a nod to the company's original name. In its first day of trading, SAIC's stock rose by 21 percent. It was a bullish open that was a sign of things to come.

The Next Evolution

As it is with any IPO, SAIC faced its share of challenges and hurdles on the way to becoming a publicly traded company. The fact that it would no longer be employee owned, a concept that was core to Beyster's business philosophy, was a major shift for a company that had long prided itself on that very ideal.

Frank Kendall is the former undersecretary of defense for acquisition, technology, and logistics. He began working with SAIC in the 1980s in Huntsville, Alabama, on missile defense projects. When he moved to the Pentagon, he continued working with the company in strategic defense,

1969

SAI

Company founder J. Robert Beyster creates an employee stock ownership program available on a sales incentive basis.

1970

SAI shares, largely held by employees, begin a steady climb, gaining an annualized compounded rate of 34 percent. An investment of $100 in 1970 was worth $3.5 million by the time of the IPO in 2006.

1995

SAIC acquires Internet domain registry Network Solutions for $4.7 million. The company is the first to offer Internet domains to the public.

1997

SAIC takes one-quarter of its ownership in Network Solutions to the market. The IPO raises $64 million, more than 10 times what SAIC had paid for the company.

missile defense, and other technical areas. After leaving government work in 1994, Kendall worked for SAIC for a short time. He is now a member of the Leidos Board of Directors. Kendall believed the company's employee ownership program worked until SAIC had become large enough that the model could no longer sustain itself. He also explained how the competitive culture within the company had to evolve in order for SAIC to continue to thrive:

The company that Bob created was very Darwinian. His basic methodology was to find smart people who wanted to do interesting things and build businesses, bring them into the company, and give them the freedom to go succeed and some resources to get started, and let them build the business within the SAIC framework. And for the first few decades of SAIC, that was very successful. But the company, I think, at some point, kind of outgrew that model. You can only have a conglomerate of so many small businesses, and what I found in the 1990s and what other people experienced too was that different parts of SAIC were as much in competition with each other as they were with other companies.

In September 2005, the SAIC Board of Directors saw an opening in the market that could be favorable for an IPO. The directors voted to launch an IPO the following year. With going public, the board imagined a future where the company could use its cash flows from operations to fund growth. Morgan Stanley & Co. and Bear, Stearns & Co. served as joint managers of the offering. The board decided that proceeds of the IPO would pay dividends to current stockholders.

While this would be the first time SAIC would go public, it wasn't the employee-owned company's first experience with IPOs. In 1995,

1997

After share prices increase on average by 19 percent over a five-year period, *Fast Company* labels SAIC's employee-ownership model "a phenomenon."

2000

Buying back employee stocks becomes a financial drain on the company. Over the next five years, it would cost $2.4 billion for SAIC to buy employee stocks, depleting the company's cash on hand and limiting expansion.

2000

SAIC sells its remaining ownership stake of Network Solutions to VeriSign for $2.6 billion, marking SAIC's purchase of the company in 1995 for $4.7 million as one of history's most profitable acquisitions.

2005

The SAIC Board of Directors votes to take the employee-owned company public for the first time.

SAIC bought Network Solutions for $4.7 million. At the time, Network Solutions had a deal with the U.S. government to register all website addresses. Two years later, SAIC took public a quarter of its stock in Network Solutions, LLC. During that opening on Sept. 27, 1997, the Network Solutions stock began trading at $18. Shares rose as much as 49 percent in the first day of trading, before ending 30 percent up at $23.31. The offering raised $64 million, more than 10 times what SAIC had paid for the company. In 2000, SAIC would sell the rest of its ownership in Network Solutions to VeriSign for a staggering $2.6 billion.

Prior to the IPO, SAIC was the country's largest employee-owned research and engineering firm, and it was also in a period of rapid growth. Revenue for the first quarter of 2005 was $1.85 billion, with $585 million in earnings, up from $89 million the prior year. The federal government was SAIC's largest customer, accounting for 86 percent of its revenue. Cash, short-term investments, and cash equivalents on hand totaled $3.19 billion. Company filings with the government valued the initial offering at $1.73 billion.

A key reason to convert SAIC to a public company was to end the firm's internal stock trading program, which allowed employee shareholders to buy and sell their shares every three months. In the previous five years, SAIC had spent $2.4 billion to purchase employee shares. Kenneth Dahlberg, then-SAIC chairman and CEO, said the program had become a financial drain on the company, keeping it from key acquisitions and spending. Buying back shares from employees consumed $500 million a year, about as much cash flow as the company saw each year.

The IPO was expected to "preserve cash flows to be used to implement our vision and strategy," Dahlberg wrote to employees, as well as to "offer

J. Robert Beyster was an authority on employee-owned companies, which he championed throughout his career and in his book, *The SAIC Solution.*

2006

2006

2006

2006

Nearly 9 out of 10 shareholders vote to approve the IPO, paving the way for it to begin.

SAIC CEO Kenneth Dahlberg rings the New York Stock Exchange bell on October 13, the first day of trading of SAIC stock.

While the era of employee ownership ends at SAIC, employees are the first to benefit from the new period in the company's history. After the IPO, employees receive $2.45 billion in dividends.

In its first day of trading under the ticker symbol "SAI," company stocks rise 21 percent.

SAIC shareholders greater liquidity for their shares should they desire to diversify their holdings." He added:

> We've been an acquirer over the history of the company. Post-IPO, we'll have the firepower to do the larger acquisitions—$200 million, $500 million and even up to billion-dollar companies.

Taking Care of Employees

For employees of SAIC, the idea of going public was a groundbreaking change. Since its founding, SAIC's culture had cemented itself around the concept of employee ownership, and longtime members of the team wondered what the future would look like for a publicly traded company. Former Chief Audit Officer Bettina García Welsh, who joined the company in 2001 as deputy controller in the SAIC office in Columbia, Maryland, explained:

> I think people were afraid to take that step. What does it mean to be public? And so we felt like an infant in the big leagues at that point in time. Here we were, quite a well-known company, and yet going into this public frame of mind and learning what it meant was very eye opening, particularly as a member of the finance leadership team and trying to help the organization be ready.

Mark Sopp came on in 2005 as the company's chief financial officer in advance of the IPO, and he had the difficult task of convincing skeptical employees that SAIC's unique culture would continue, and even improve,

2007

Despite the complicated IPO, SAIC announces a return of 11.9 percent for the previous year.

2007

Post-public offering, SAIC sees unprecedented growth, with 9,000 active federal contracts worth over $1 billion.

2007

SAIC has 44,000 staff members and is larger than the U.S. Departments of Energy, Labor, and Housing and Urban Development— combined. By this year, the company has won more individual government contracts than any other U.S. private company in history.

2009

SAIC relocates its headquarters from San Diego to McLean, Virginia, in a move to consolidate its corporate structure and keep employees closer to Washington, D.C.

A CROSS-COUNTRY RELOCATION

After four decades of calling San Diego home, in 2009 SAIC officially moved its corporate headquarters to McLean, Virginia. Already, the company had 17,500 employees in the Washington, D.C. area. But the decision meant that some of the 4,500 employees the company had in San Diego County would relocate to the new headquarters by 2013, including administrative, finance, and legal functions. San Diego would continue to serve as a technology hub for the company.

The move came as the company restructured the management style from the decentralized system it had maintained since its founding into one with a more centralized model. "Virginia's favorable business environment, highly skilled workforce, and attractive quality of life combine to make this an ideal location for our corporate headquarters," said former CEO Walt Havenstein.

Mark Sopp, former chief financial officer and executive vice president, said the move presented a substantial challenge. SAIC not only had to suddenly set up entire departments on another coast, but, complicating the process, Havenstein left during the transition. He was replaced with retired U.S. Air Force General John Jumper, who saw the move as imperative. "We kind of moved the flag, but we retained a big presence in San Diego, so that wasn't too painful," Sopp said. "But when General Jumper joined, he really wanted to go all in, if you will, and get out of San Diego, and so there was a quite sudden requirement to completely exit San Diego from a corporate perspective, and that was very challenging."

after going public. "It was a very significant challenge for sure," said Sopp. "There were a number of folks in the company that were not supportive of going public, and there was a whole culture that was focused on cannibalistic growth, so to speak, and not so much focused on profits and cash flow and, inevitably, the distribution of cash to people other than the employees, such as third-party shareholders." Sopp added:

> *The more challenging part was to convince folks that it was good business to negotiate tough and to improve profitability while not damaging customer intimacy and relationships. And also to build the internal mechanisms to prosecute the business in a more automated, repeatable, standard way, which we spent a lot of time doing leading up to the IPO, but more significantly, afterwards, actually, over the following two, three years. I spent a lot of time on the wiring and the process to make it standard, repeatable, and automated.*

Most privately owned companies that go public use the money that's raised to increase business. The potential billions that SAIC's public offering would raise could have drastically increased its reach. But throughout the IPO process, the Board of Directors made clear the employee owners would stand to benefit. SAIC's employees received special dividends for their company shares, and they would also subsequently receive stock in the newly formed public company. After the IPO, those employees would be among the existing shareholders to retain 80 percent of SAIC capital stock and 98 percent of the voting power. To reassure employees that the plan was in their best interest, Dahlberg issued a video address on September 2, 2005, to clarify how the employees would benefit.

The timing of the IPO was, in fact, fortuitous for the employee shareholders, and received a great deal of industry and media attention at the time. Industry valuations in 2005 were relatively at a peak, said Larry Davis, managing partner of the merger and acquisitions advisory firm Aronson Capital Partners LLC in Rockville, Maryland. Also advantageous for the company's IPO was a *Vanity Fair* article published about SAIC. The article described the company's deep involvement in secretive government programs. While those confidential arrangements complicated the IPO, keeping the company from releasing the kind of information other public offerings might include, it also seemed to increase SAIC's value, as Sopp explained:

> *I think that the public found it intriguing and mysterious that we were so heavily involved in things we couldn't talk about, and that led to the mystique of the IPO itself. There was just this mystique of being*

The bull tramples the bear in a trophy Nelson Chai, then-executive vice president and chief financial officer of NYSE Group, gave to SAIC's CEO Kenneth C. Dahlberg ahead of the company's first day of trading.

such a large, private company involved in so many secretive and important things that there was some euphoria, if you will. Plus, we did a good job, I think, selling the company and the IPO, and that warranted a good price, but we had to earn it the hard way over time, which we did.

The Board of Directors' plan went to the shareholders for a vote on September 27, 2006, at a shareholder meeting in McLean, Virginia. More than 86 percent of the shareholders voted to go ahead with the IPO.

Opening Bell

Above: The ceremonial gavel given to CEO Ken Dahlberg after the SAIC stockholder approval of establishing an IPO on September 27, 2006.

Below: The SAIC flag hangs outside the New York Stock Exchange on the day the company went public on October 13, 2006.

Following the IPO, employees would retain control of SAIC, owning 81 percent of the stock at the time the company went public. Since each employee share counted as 10 votes each, that meant employees held 98 percent of voting power. It also meant employees stood to gain financially. Those with longevity in the company and retirees who had held on to their stocks through the years stood to see substantial windfalls.

The company's value had been rising steadily since its founding in 1969. The employees who owned shares would also earn a portion of the money the company raised from the IPO through a special dividend.

After decades of employee ownership, SAIC scheduled October 13, 2006, as the day it would go public. The night before, its board of directors met to set the initial public offering price and decide the amount of dividend the

HOW EMPLOYEES HANDLED THE IPO

For employees of a company that had lived by the mantra, "I own because I care, and I care because I own," it was important to staff members to continue to live by that pledge, even as the company went public. Eventually, employees would no longer own enough stock to maintain control of the company, but the culture of employee ownership would remain, thanks to the selfless guidance of the company's leaders and board members. "We made sure that all of our core values stayed in place," said retired U.S. Marine Major General Arnold Punaro, former SAIC executive vice president and general manager for Washington operations. "We helped employees avoid any unnecessary concerns by keeping them fully informed."

It also helped that those who owned stocks stood to benefit from the IPO. Newer employees received more modest sums from the dividends paid out after the stock offering, but some long-term employees and retirees saw life-changing checks. As a colonel with the U.S. Army Corps of Engineers, Ralph Sievers (pictured) designed and carried out above- and below-ground nuclear weapon effects testing in Nevada in 1958. When he retired in 1977, he joined SAIC the following day and then retired from the company in 1996. Over his two decades of service to the company, Sievers not only received stocks as bonuses, but he also invested in SAIC,

believing rightly that the company stock would see increases.

After the IPO, Sievers was told he would receive a sizeable check in the mail. "I tried to get the people to do a fund transfer because I didn't really want to see a large check in the mail," Sievers said. "But I received it on a Friday afternoon. I had a family funeral to go to out of town for the weekend, so I had this $8 million check in my pocket until Monday morning."

Today, Sievers is one the of largest individual shareholders of the company.

company would pay to existing stockholders. The board set the offering price at $15 per share and approved a special cash dividend totaling $2.45 billion.

On the morning of October 13, SAIC CEO Ken Dahlberg rang the opening bell from above the New York Stock Exchange trading floor. Already, SAIC had sold 75 million shares to mutual funds and other investors, raising $1.1 billion. With that valuation, the company entered public trading with a worth of $6 billion.

In its first day of trading, SAIC's stock saw an immediate jump. From the initial price of $15, the stock rose 21 percent by the close of trading, to $18.18 per share. In total, the company's public offering raised just over $1 billion. After SAIC's first successful day as a publicly traded company, the firm was off to the races and never looked back.

Keeping the Spirit of Employee Ownership

Throughout the IPO process, SAIC management feared the process could become a distraction for employees. Well before the IPO's completion, management knew they would have to begin the work of restructuring SAIC to turn it into a public company. To counteract the damage that could have resulted from both processes, the company took quick measures.

Employees were encouraged to concentrate on day-to-day operations rather than the ins and outs of the IPO and the ups and downs of the market. Stuart Davis, then a senior vice president of investor relations for the company, took over the job of disseminating information to employees

Opposite top:
A monitor at the New York Stock Exchange previews SAIC's first day of trading.

Opposite bottom:
The New York Stock Exchange's gilded conference room was used to celebrate SAIC's public offering.

Left: Employees were the first to benefit from SAIC's public offering, receiving dividends for the stocks they owned.

The trading bell on October 13, 2006, is rung by SAIC's CEO, Kenneth C. Dahlberg.

and outside investors. "A big part of my job is to keep employees informed so they can continue to focus on operations," Davis said. To help this effort, the company established call centers to help educate employees on the IPO process.

Today, Leidos continues to have a hotline where employees can call to ask questions or to report various concerns. Melissa Koskovich, Leidos' senior vice president and director of communications and marketing, explained how the hotline has evolved over the years to serve its employees:

> Well beyond the IPO process, the call center persists thanks to a corporate culture that's different from other companies. Here at Leidos, we have this cultural departure where we believe the CEO works for every employee. He's not here to run everybody around. One example of that is our ethics and compliance hotline. At other companies, the majority of employees that call in are anonymous. Here, the majority leave their name, and they want somebody to call them back to explain why such and such is going on at the company.

The measures SAIC took to ensure the public offering went smoothly worked far better than anyone could have predicted. In the year following the IPO, the company reported annual revenue of $8.3 billion, a 7 percent increase. Operating income rose 19 percent.

Sopp, who served as the company's chief financial officer and executive vice president from 2005–2015, described how the IPO process allowed the company to begin thinking about business in ways it had never done previously:

> *During the IPO process, for the very first time, we developed a long-term forecast, which the company had never done. We told the public we would grow revenues at double the pace than we had previously done in the couple of years leading up to the IPO. We told the public that we would increase profitability by 20 to 30 basis points per year and we would generate earnings per share growth of 15 percent. Any one of those three is pretty hard to do. We told the Street we'd do all three at the same time, and the reason why we were in favor with the investment community, at least in the first few years after going public, is we met those targets precisely for three to four years. And I think SAIC as a whole should have been very justifiably proud of that because that was a huge amount of operational improvement from when it was private, at least the years leading up to the IPO when it was private.*

Mark Sopp served as SAIC's chief financial officer and executive vice president during the company's IPO.

Quite simply, new growth occurred because the company brought in a tremendous amount of new business. Among the new business was a $394 million U.S. Air Force contract for command and control-related work. Additionally, NATO awarded SAIC a $95 million contract to provide services surrounding ballistic missile defense capabilities.

By 2007, SAIC had 44,000 staff members and was larger than the U.S. Departments of Energy, Labor, and Housing and Urban Development—combined. The company had won more individual government contracts than any other U.S. private company in history, and at the time, two of the company's 9,000 active federal contracts were worth over $1 billion. More than 100 of those contracts with the U.S. government topped $10 million. In 2006, SAIC posted a return of 11.9 percent, higher than ExxonMobil. With the IPO behind it, the company set its sights on a new goal: $12 billion in revenue by 2008.

Today at Leidos, many who were with the company before the IPO believe Beyster's vision of employee ownership has survived as a result of the entrepreneurial foundation that remains. "We still have this entrepreneurial spirit," said Chuck Fralick, maritime solutions architect for the company's advanced solutions work. "I bet if you looked across the spectrum of defense and health services companies, nobody matches us head to head. That's a legacy of the way the company started, which is very entrepreneurial, employee owned. We just attracted the best people, and we still do." ■

CHAPTER TEN

LEIDOS IS BORN

The whole idea behind creating two new companies was for both entities to gain access to additional markets, to expand, and to decrease our cost structure.

───────────

John P. Jumper
RETIRED U.S. AIR FORCE GENERAL AND
FORMER LEIDOS CHAIRMAN AND CEO

A FTER 44 YEARS IN OPERATION, SAIC WOULD UNDERGO A MASSIVE change in 2013 that would split the firm into two separate companies. One would be dedicated to government services, a new $4 billion firm that would be known as the new SAIC. The legacy company would be dedicated to solutions, a $6 billion company that would be named Leidos. Retired U.S. Air Force General John P. Jumper would serve as the chairman and CEO of Leidos, and the company would relocate its corporate headquarters to Reston, Virginia.

There was a lot to lose for the company as a result of the split. At the time, SAIC was ranked No. 5 among the top 100 technology companies in Washington. It handled $6 billion in prime contracts and had more than $11 billion in total revenue. A misstep in the separation would have caused a distraction among the employees that could cost the company major contracts. "When we finally started bringing everybody into the fold, we were very specific with our employees," SAIC's then-chief operating officer, K. Stuart Shea, said at the time. "We told them that 99 percent of the people in the company needed to stay focused on delivering to our customers. That was absolutely imperative."

It would take a tremendous amount of coordination, customer education, and employee resilience to solidify the separation and ensure that it

Opposite: Logo
installation on
Freedom Square 1,
part of the Leidos
headquarters in
Reston, Virginia.

went smoothly. Thanks to that work, Leidos came out of the parting a stronger company able to adapt quickly to customer needs and to stay on the leading edge of technological innovation.

Pursuing New Opportunities

The idea and discussions to split the company into two separate entities first surfaced in February 2012. By August of that year, the SAIC board voted to further evaluate the split, and on August 30, company executives made the plan public. The board expected the separation would occur sometime between July 2013 and January 2014.

Signing ceremony for the separation agreement on September 23, 2013, which formalized the creation of Leidos and the spinoff of SAIC. Back row (left to right) are Doug Wagoner and Vincent Maffeo. Front row (left to right) are Ray Veldman, John Jumper, and Charlie Kanewske.

2012

SAIC executives begin planning to split the 44-year-old company into two separate entities.

2012

A team of 50 employees begins working on the split, a plan that is internally dubbed "Project Gemini."

2012

The separation of the two companies is announced publicly.

2013

The SAIC Board of Directors officially votes to split the company in two and approves a stock dividend to spin off new SAIC to shareholders.

The SAIC Board of Directors would also be split among the two companies. Board members France A. Cordova, Jere A. Drummond, Thomas F. Frist III, and Edward J. Sanderson Jr. would become directors of the board at the new, spun-off SAIC. SAIC board members Miriam E. John, Anita K. Jones, John P. Jumper, Harry M. J. Kraemer Jr., and Lawrence C. Nussdorf would remain on the board of the legacy company that would be renamed Leidos. Following the distribution, David G. Fubini, Robert S. Shapard, and Noel A. Williams would also join the Leidos board.

After more than four decades in operation, SAIC officially split into two companies on September 27, 2013. Leidos would become a $6 billion solutions-focused business and SAIC would focus its efforts as a $4 billion services business.

SAIC and Leidos shared a co-branded trade show booth at AUSA Annual 2013, the first customer-facing event following the company's split.

Allowing Both Companies to Thrive

Before the split, SAIC had encountered multiple contracts it had to pass on due to conflicts of interest. Often, one SAIC division would have to bow out of a project it was well suited to take on because another division in the company had provided Systems Engineering and Technical Assistance (SETA) to the customer. "The whole idea was for both entities to gain access to additional markets, to expand, and to decrease our cost structure," Jumper said. "We can completely remove our conflict of interest, which for Leidos

2013   **2013**   **2014**   **2014**

FEBRUARY

The company announces the new name for the company, Leidos, derived from the word kaleidoscope, "a memorable word with dynamic connotations," said Stu Shea, who would serve as chief operating officer of Leidos.

SEPTEMBER 27

With the stroke of a pen, two companies agree to separate—the $4 billion services business known as SAIC, and the $6 billion solutions-focused business, now named Leidos.

CEO General John P. Jumper announces his retirement. He will stay on board while Leidos searches for a new leader.

The Leidos Board of Directors hires veteran executive Roger Krone as the company's new CEO.

opens opportunities of about $37 billion a year that we didn't have before."

Beyond resolving SETA conflicts, splitting the companies meant more efficiency in managing distinct portions of the businesses differently, which allowed the two firms to make additional competitive offerings. The new companies could differentiate their solutions and systems for specific customers, rather than creating products to fulfill multiple client needs. With greater market share, the split would create more growth potential for employees. Investors also saw a benefit in a greater understanding of the two companies and their focus on distinct market sectors.

Deborah Lee James, former secretary of the U.S. Air Force and the former president of the SAIC Technology and Engineering Sector, was involved in the process to shape the new SAIC. James' team decided how to structure the new company and the approach it would take in the future, which she explained:

Outgoing SAIC President and CEO General John Jumper signing the official papers for the separation of Leidos from SAIC.

> There certainly was give and take along the way. The approach that we ended up taking for the new SAIC in terms of structure and organization was quite a bit different from the old SAIC. Specifically, what we chose for the new SAIC was a matrix management type of approach where you would have customer-focused groups and then you would have capability-focused groups. So, for example, a customer-focused group might be the Army customer group or the Navy customer group or the civil agency-focused group. And then examples of the capabilities groups might be software engineering or hard-

2014

Krone begins a plan to remove the distractions of the corporate separation and return Leidos employees to the task of developing innovative technical solutions and supporting customers.

2014

Leidos directs employees and resources toward a potentially major contract with the Pentagon to upgrade its internal healthcare system, a program known as the Defense Healthcare Management System Modernization, or DHMSM.

2014

The new Leidos website launches with more than 1,000 rebranded pages. Within three months, the award-winning site sees 300,000 visits.

2014

DECEMBER 22

SAIC founder J. Robert Beyster passes away at the age of 90.

ware or vehicle integration. So these are different capabilities that we had, and then the idea was: If the Army-focused customer group needed that software team, they would be matrixed in, but then three months later, maybe the Navy group would need them, and so they would leave the Army group and they would go where they were needed.

SAIC, the smaller of the two companies, would primarily focus on the government sector, delivering repeatable solutions including IT and technical services. Leidos, even with the new name and branding, was the original SAIC, and retained much of the company's upper management team, along with rights to the company's history. For Leidos, 30 percent of its revenue would be derived from the commercial sector. The company would be focused on innovative technologies in specific sectors, including engineering, health, and national security. These specialties would have an underlying technical thread linking each of the sectors, highlighting the firm's specialty of sophisticated analytics and large amounts of data.

Melissa Koskovich, Leidos' senior vice president and director of Communications and Marketing, was one of the key members of the team figuring out how to split SAIC. Koskovich said the team began with the idea that they were creating two world-class companies that would both last another 50 years. She explained the vision for each company going forward:

> *Our goal was not just to make Leidos a success; it was to make both companies successful. At the time, those government entities that were working with what is now the new SAIC, placed a lot of importance on the strong recognition of the SAIC name that we all knew in the past. Meanwhile, Leidos had commercial businesses and civil markets that we had aspired to broaden into, and also international hopes for the future.*

Melissa Koskovich, senior vice president and director, Communications and Marketing for Leidos.

2015

The Pentagon awards Leidos the DHMSM contract, worth at least $4.3 billion.

2018

Goldman Sachs adds Leidos to its "conviction list," with the company's free cash flow per share expected to grow 40 percent in 2018, 30 percent in 2019, and 15 percent in 2020.

2018

CREDIT: PHOTO COURTESY OF RISDON PHOTOGRAPHY.

FEBRUARY

General John P. Jumper announces his retirement from the Leidos Board of Directors in February, after 11 years with the company.

2018

Forbes recognizes Leidos as one of America's Best Employers.

So it made sense at the time to evaluate and decide that SAIC would go to the company that was going to stay in our traditional markets. And then the company that had the larger aspirations was going to embark on the journey to have a new name.

The two separate entities would enter a slew of agreements to split up assets; among them, the new SAIC would remain headquartered in McLean, Virginia, while Leidos would establish its headquarters nearby in Reston.

Rounding Out the Process

Splitting the company also meant operations that did not align well would be divided between the new companies, allowing both the new SAIC and Leidos to have a more clear focus. "It's to change ourselves from what was 1,000 flowers blooming, a company [still rooted] in employee ownership with hundreds of operations that were not well coordinated, into one that can share technology across the enterprise," said General Jumper in a *Washington Business Journal* article. "The separation allows us to break the rubber band."

Mark Sopp, the chief financial officer at the time of the split, says it was a difficult process to choose a name, and for many it became a major issue discussed at length. But Sopp said for Leidos employees, they simply needed

The company changed its ticker symbol to LDOS in 2013.
(Used with permission of NYSE Group, Inc., ©2017.)

to concentrate on what had always made the company successful. "I was always of the view that we can choose any variety of things, and it's probably not going to matter a whole lot," Sopp said. "As long as we deliver for our customers and build a culture of performance and excellence and treat our people well, whatever we call ourselves, the public will eventually latch on."

In September 2013, the SAIC board officially approved a stock dividend of new SAIC shares to the company's stockholders. Each SAIC, Inc. stockholder would receive seven shares of new SAIC for every share of SAIC, Inc. they owned. SAIC would then change its name to Leidos Holdings, Inc., and on the New York Stock Exchange change its ticker symbol to LDOS. The board also approved a one-for-four reverse stock split of Leidos shares that would take effect immediately after the distribution. In a corporate press release, General Jumper said of the split:

> *SAIC has a proud legacy of solving complex problems, thriving on innovation and working shoulder-to-shoulder with customers. For the next chapter, we will take things to the next level—moving forward and launching two great American companies that will continue to serve the best interests of not only our customers and shareholders, but also our communities, our families, and our world.*

Welcome Roger Krone

Immediately after the split, Leidos experienced unrelated challenges that led to a downturn analysts and corporate executives did not expect. During the final quarter of 2013, revenue had fallen 15 percent from the year before,

Activities in the Reston Town Center pavilion celebrate the IPO and official launch of Leidos at its new headquarters in Reston, Virginia, on September 30, 2013.

Former CEO General John Jumper, left, with new Leidos CEO Roger Krone at an employee town hall event on July 16, 2014.

and the company expected an operating loss of 7 million, compared to income of $100 million from the previous year. In the second quarter of 2014, Leidos posted a loss of $438 million due to goodwill impairment charges.

Earlier in February of that year, General Jumper announced his retirement. The new company began a search for his successor. During the transition, General Jumper would remain at the helm and as chairman of the board. "I brought to the company the skills that I have at the right time [and] at the right place," General Jumper said to the *Washington Post* at the time. "Now it's time to really transition to someone who can drive the financial results and brings a career full of business experience."

After an exhaustive search of potential CEO candidates, the Leidos Board of Directors hired Roger Krone to lead the new company. He would replace General Jumper on July 14, 2014. Krone was a 1978 graduate of Georgia Tech, where he earned his bachelor's degree in aerospace engineering. He then earned a master's degree in aerospace engineering from the University of Texas at Arlington, and a Master of Business Administration from the Harvard Graduate School of Business. Krone spent 14 years at General Dynamics before becoming director of financial planning at McDonnell Douglas in 1992. In 1997, he served as vice president and treasurer of McDonnell Douglas during its merger with The Boeing Company. Later, as president of Boeing's space and network systems, Krone oversaw 15,000 employees in 35 states and 12 countries. Among the projects he oversaw were Boeing's Army systems, which included the Apache and Chinook helicopter programs.

At the time, Krone described his challenge as the new CEO of Leidos as a financial one, and said his background was well suited to put Leidos on the correct path. "Any time you split a company, it's a challenge," Krone said. "But that was a year ago. Me coming in—it completes the set of moves that the board had in mind to put us on solid foundation."

Krone also knew that the company had to get beyond the split and the name change and all the attention that had been given to it. It needed to focus on core principles and a new guiding mission, as he described:

> *We're in the branding journey on Leidos. So what we'll establish with the name is not whether we picked a catchy word or we made up a name. It's the performance that we deliver to our customers, and the people that stand behind the name that matters. It takes five years to build a brand, and people now know who we are. We've recently redone our mission, our vision, and our values to make what we stand for clearer, but we still have work to do in*

building the brand. Purple is a great color, and people have really gotten excited over it. If you walk around the company, you see everybody has embraced the color. I think Melissa [Koskovich] and her team have done a great job of building the brand, and I would say we make her job easier when our execution and program performance is superior. At the end of the day, our customers look to us to deliver on our commitments and to help them execute their mission.

A Continued Vision

In the role of CEO at Leidos, Krone had an immediate vision for the company. He described a simple strategy to remove distractions and allow Leidos' experts to return to the important work they knew best.

Krone knew the company's investments in the national security sector had paid off and the federal healthcare business continued to grow. Those areas helped offset losses elsewhere, and Krone believed that concentrating on them would help elevate the other divisions until they returned to profitability. "We need to invest in things like research and development, continued innovation, and internal collaboration, and we need to take care

Creating the Leidos brand meant rebranding externally and internally, like this fifth-floor mural at the company's headquarters, located in Reston, Virginia.

Leidos initiated a three-year sponsorship with the DC United soccer team to expand its international brand identity. Pictured right: Krone greets DC United Mascot "Talon" during the 2014 Leidos Leadership Summit.

of our people—they are the ones that will drive this company forward," Krone said. "If we can do all of those things and be competitive in our markets, we will continue to have a strong business in the future."

In July 2015, just months after Krone helped steer the company toward its new goals, the Pentagon awarded Leidos a massive $4.3 billion health system contract. The Defense Healthcare Management Systems Modernization (DHMSM) contract, now known as MHS GENESIS, would span at least a decade and could continue for an additional eight years, at a total value of $9 billion. More than 1,200 sites, including hospitals and other healthcare facilities, will eventually use the software.

While Krone mostly kept the company focused on work within its proven areas of expertise, he also steered the company into new waters, which earned him several accolades. For instance, in February 2018, *Federal Computer Week* named Krone to its Federal 100 list. The annual award recognizes leaders from academics, industry, or government who have made significant contributions to the government's information technology efforts.

According to General Jumper, the major contracts the company secured after the split are evidence that the move was necessary and beneficial:

> *I think the recent wins we have had on a big contract in the U.K. and a big contract with the Department of Defense on the health side, shows that we did the right thing. It was the right thing to do, no matter how hard it was, and we've come out in a position where we are truly configured as a public company. We have shared services. We have the right kind of centralized operation that takes advantage of efficiencies and things that, in SAIC, were much more difficult to do with the employee-owned legacy of the company.*

Evolving the Company Into the Future

With the SAIC spin-off complete, the newly formed Leidos had to create its own corporate identity, nearly from scratch. Although the firm was 44 years old, it had to almost start over again in building its brand. The trick was to share the story of a company that was both an established inside-the-beltway government contractor and also a nimble startup, ready to take on the technological challenges of tomorrow.

The effort to brand Leidos actually began in 2012, long before the two companies split. To create this new vision, executives at SAIC partnered with Interbrand, a brand consultancy firm with previous work with corporations such as Bing, Dunkin' Donuts, and Porsche. Interbrand conducted about 50 interviews with then-SAIC employees before dreaming up 3,400 possibilities for new names and brand identities. The agency considered metaphors that could convey a company ethos of achieving things that might have before seemed impossible. It considered a comparison to the space race or the Olympics or some other great competition. After 18 months of work, company officials selected a concept of a kaleidoscope, a metaphor of the various divisions and skills of the company coming together in one ever-adaptable vision. Clipped from the word kaleidoscope, Leidos was born.

WHAT'S IN A NAME?

Although the company had operated under the name SAIC for more than 40 years, a new name was born when the two firms went their separate ways. The company hired branding expert Interbrand to help develop the new name.

Interbrand executives conducted 50 interviews with SAIC employees, who themselves were combing trademarked names in dozens of countries to make sure ideas were not already taken.

In the end, the name Leidos was selected. It comes from the center of the word "kaleidoscope," reflecting the firm's goal of bringing together solutions from all different angles.

As part of the process of selecting a new name, the company had to make sure any option they considered wasn't already trademarked, recalled Ray Veldman, senior vice president, deputy general counsel, and corporate secretary of Leidos. "We had to do trademark searches, not only in the United States, but in every country where we did business. So that was an exhaustive process and we also had to look for domain name registrations, and what we found out was most of the names that we looked at that we liked were already in use. So that was maybe one of the most frustrating parts of the transaction, and because the name was new, nobody liked whatever name we were going to come up with. But it's since grown on us, and I think everybody's happy with the Leidos name."

Next, the company had to select a logo, and Interbrand came up with 10 options. The company settled on what is referred to as the Vertex, an angular symbol constructed from two different-colored two-dimensional planes. Each plane, and the angles and colors created from its intersections, represents the different groups and capabilities within Leidos. Depending on the angle of viewing, a new idea and a new color form, symbolizing the full breadth and power of Leidos.

Leidos also chose purple as a principal color, rare in the corporate world, especially among defense contractors. The new name, logo, and color scheme received a "grand unveiling" before the split occurred. For months

The SAIC signage comes down on the Roger Bacon Drive building in Reston, Virginia, in preparation for the new Leidos name going up in its place.

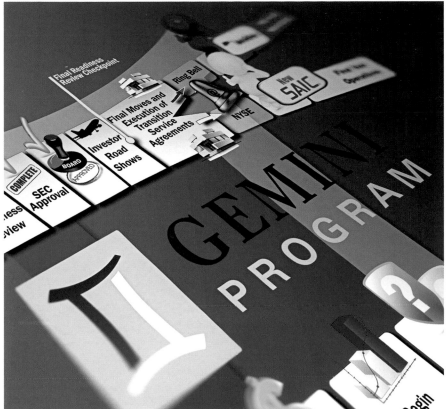

Left: At the outset, Project Gemini simply named the two companies White Co. and Blue Co., with Wagoner assigning employees to each team and developing the new Leidos brand before completing the transaction to spin off SAIC.

Below: Doug Wagoner, former president of the Services and Solutions sector at SAIC, helped oversee the split, which internally took on the code-name Project Gemini.

afterward, the two companies would operate as one under the same roof until the split became official. Then the new logo of Leidos would rise onto its new Reston headquarters.

"The idea of rebranding a company is far more complicated than it might look from the outside," Koskovich said. After designing the logo and color palette, Leidos would need to replace every SAIC logo and the color blue on everything from hallway walls to business cards to building floor maps, as Koskovich described:

> We really started from nothing, and when you start from nothing, you realize the importance of getting your building blocks right, and we had to move quickly. With a deadline approaching of the company's separation, the new logo and color scheme had to be everywhere before the separation occurred. So we had to very quickly take the logo that we created and get it out to the masses, in every form imaginable.

Doug Wagoner, former president of the Services and Solutions sector at SAIC, joined the company in 2007. He helped oversee the separation of the two companies, which internally took on the name Project Gemini. At the beginning of Project Gemini, Wagoner recalled that his team simply named the two companies White Co. and Blue Co., assigning employees to them and working on the branding, before settling on the names of each.

On January 20, 2016, Leidos helped sponsor Military Appreciation Night at the Verizon Center, during a Washington Wizards basketball game.

When the name Leidos had been decided, the team sent an e-mail to employees on a Sunday night and set up a new Project Gemini e-mail to field responses. At first, the responses were overwhelmingly negative. "Then people went into negotiation. 'Hey, shouldn't we vote on this? I think the board of directors needs to approve this.' Yes, they did. And then by Friday of that week, it was: 'Well, it kind of makes sense,' and, 'Well, I guess it's not that bad of a name.' But, one, it was the sense of loss, that they had lost the SAIC name, and then the name that they got was a very different kind of name in Leidos," Wagoner recalled. "And I think a lot of people had a hard time with that, and they also were mostly engineers, and engineers don't deal well with the abstract. That's not what they deal with. And Leidos is a very abstract name, so that was the one thing that created more emotion than anything else by far, was the name."

Stuart Crawford, who spent 17 years with the company and managed the United Kingdom's air traffic management programs, said an initial challenge with the Leidos name was receiving recognition among customers. Now, looking toward the next decade, it has become a benefit. "From a U.K. perspective, I've got to say that Leidos was not an instantly recognizable, well-known brand," Crawford said. "I sense that that's changing and, actually, perhaps quicker than I ever thought it would. People I speak to within the industry and particularly in some of the recruitment organizations located here within London—they see Leidos as being a real positive, disruptive force moving forward."

For customers, the name Leidos has developed a connection to the advanced solutions and technological prowess the company possesses. That's the experience of Walter Harris, the current vice president for operations and chief operating officer at George Washington University's School of Medicine & Health Sciences, where he interacts with Leidos to create partnerships between industry and the university. Previously, Harris interacted with Leidos in his role as deputy commissioner for operations and as the chief operating officer for the U.S. Food and Drug Administration (FDA), overseeing 17,000 employees and a $4.8 billion budget. There, Harris had worked with Leidos in the development of the MARCS system, which allows for FDA data-sharing applications, inspections, and reviews to be done in concert with the agency's industry partners. When Harris came to the FDA in 2012, the program was experiencing a lot of problems. After a competitive bid, Leidos took over the MARCS system and converted it into an efficient, effective tool for the government and industry partners. Harris acknowledged that this work is synonymous with what Leidos has come to be known for accomplishing. "I like the fact that they didn't come in with glossy slides bragging about how many projects they've worked on," said Harris. "They actually came in the door having done their homework, having studied my problems at the FDA. They came in the door with my problem on the table. Something I've thought about that keeps me up at night, they've already thought about to help me through the issue."

As it was when J. Robert Beyster founded SAI, the company never relied on a name, branding, or even on its past accomplishments to pave the way for future success. Instead, Beyster believed the company would always have a seat at the table as long as it continued to provide past and future customers with advanced, efficient, and, many times, disruptive problem-solving solutions. ∎

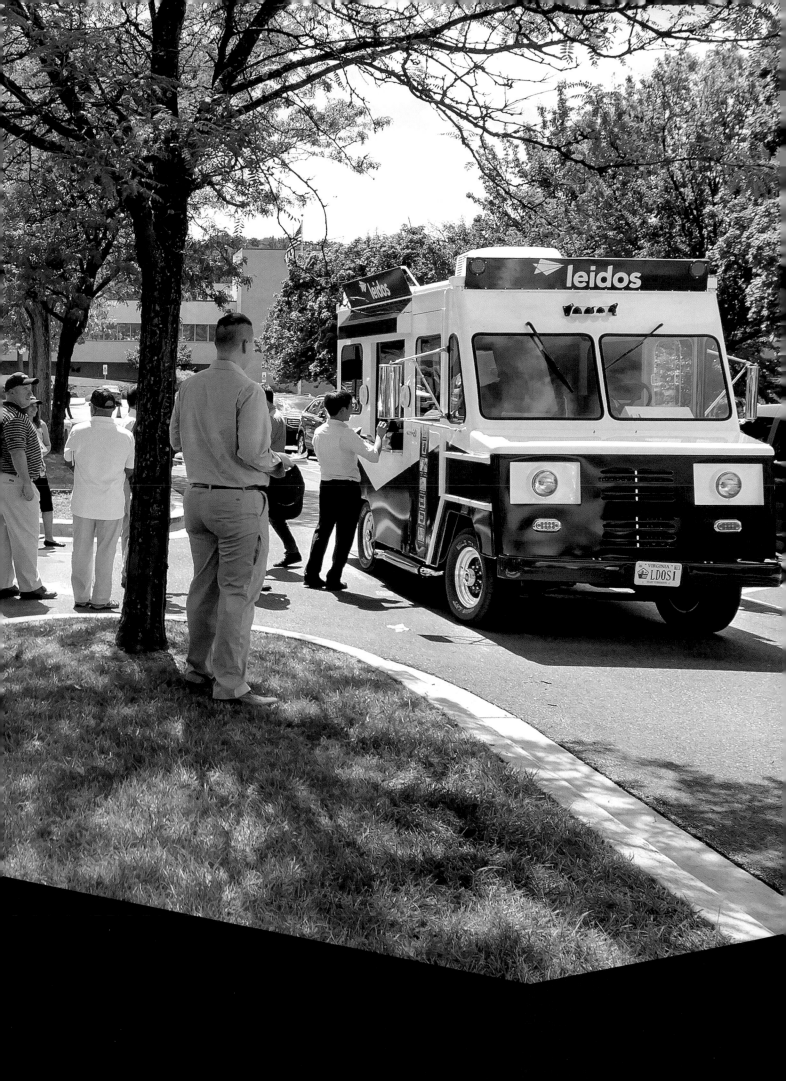

CHAPTER ELEVEN

WELCOME IS&GS

The possibility for the future really is enabled by how well we've been integrating the IS&GS business so far, and by the time we're finished, we will be ready to take on another new challenge, and I'm sure that those opportunities will be coming along sometime in the near future.

James Reagan
LEIDOS CHIEF FINANCIAL OFFICER

L OCKHEED MARTIN'S FORMER INFORMATION SYSTEMS & GLOBAL Solutions (IS&GS) business was a behemoth in providing government services, and with some 16,000 employees all over the world, the business unit was known for its stellar reputation of expertise and professionalism. With Leidos not too far from the Maryland-based firm, which had $5 billion in annual sales, the two organizations had a meeting of the minds, and on August 16, 2016, Leidos completed its merger with IS&GS.

When combined, the two would strongly complement one another, and folding the IS&GS business into Leidos' operations fit like a hand in a glove. "Today marks the next step in the evolution of Leidos," said Chairman and CEO Roger Krone on the first day of the new, combined company. "I'm excited about where we came from and what the future holds."

With the acquisition of IS&GS, Leidos would become the largest company in the government services industry at the time, nearly doubling the revenue of its closest competitors. Combined, Leidos and IS&GS were expected to see $1.2 billion in cost savings and would bring together approximately $10 billion in yearly revenue.

IS&GS had been a leading government service provider for decades, so following the deal, Leidos expanded to 33,000 employees across its locations in 30 countries. Of the 16,100 IS&GS employees, 12,000 were engineers, professionals, scientists, and technicians, and more than 5,500 held security clearances.

Opposite: Leidos acquired and restored a 1969 Ford Good Humor Ice Cream truck from the same year the company was founded. The truck, named "The Leidos Scoop," was used to serve ice cream to employees during the Day One celebrations.

Vince Maffeo served as Leidos general counsel through the company's IS&GS transaction.

Why IS&GS?

After the effects of the 2013 spin-off of the new SAIC settled, the new leadership at Leidos began to seriously think about potential growth opportunities within its areas of expertise, not just organically, but through mergers and acquisitions. The perfect opportunity Leidos was searching for arrived in the summer of 2015 when Lockheed Martin announced that it would be divesting the bulk of its IS&GS business. "Lockheed Martin had a business that was in a lot of the same markets that we were in, but we didn't compete head to head in a lot of areas," said Vince Maffeo, Leidos' then-general counsel, who added:

> *There was a tremendous amount of complementarity between what Lockheed Martin [IS&GS] was doing and what we were doing, and that suggested to us that, if we were to figure out a way to combine these resources, we could not only expand our market significantly, but we could also do it in a way that wouldn't cannibalize anything we were already doing because there wasn't much overlap. So there was a lot of attractiveness about getting together with Lockheed Martin [IS&GS].*

Building the Team

To complete the deal, Leidos used what is known as a Reverse Morris Trust transaction that would have Lockheed Martin create a subsidiary out of its IS&GS division, with which Leidos would then merge. Lockheed Martin shareholders received approximately 50.5 percent of the new combined Leidos on a diluted basis. The balance would be held by pre-transaction

2002

Lockheed Martin's IS&GS begins work on the Command, Control, Battle Management, and Communications (C2BMC) contract with the Missile Defense Agency.

2009

IS&GS becomes the lead parent company for Mission Support Alliance at the Hanford nuclear cleanup site. The contract is expected to last 10 years and cost $3 billion.

2011

CREDIT: UNITED STATES ANTARCTIC PROGRAM, NATIONAL SCIENCE FOUNDATION BY PHOTOGRAPHER RACHEL MURRAY.)

IS&GS wins a $2 billion contract with the National Science Foundation to provide support and maintenance for the U.S. Antarctic Program.

2012

IS&GS wins a $980 million follow-on C2BMC contract and would go on to win another follow-on worth $870 million in 2015.

Leidos shareholders. Lockheed Martin would receive a cash payment of about $1.8 billion to bring the total value of the transaction to $5 billion. Pre-transaction shareholders of Leidos would receive a special dividend of $1 billion that would be funded in part by new borrowing and the company's cash on hand.

Krone would continue as chairman and CEO of the newly combined company and James Reagan would continue as chief financial officer. Lockheed Martin would then designate three new directors to serve on the Leidos board and bring with it IS&GS senior staff to help augment the

Leidos Chief Financial Officer James Reagan and then-Leidos Chief Human Resources Officer Ann Addison speak to new Leidos employees during Day One celebration activities on August 16, 2016, in Gaithersburg, Maryland, following the merger of Lockheed Martin's IS&GS business with Leidos.

2012

The Defense Information Systems Agency awards IS&GS the Global Information Grid Services Management Operations contract with a $1.9 billion ceiling over seven years.

2016

AUGUST 16

Leidos completes its acquisition of IS&GS. Senior Leidos executives begin the work to integrate the two companies into one unit.

2017

Becoming the largest pure play IT services company in the industry, Leidos sets its sights on much larger IT contracts, including the U.S. Navy's Next Generation Enterprise Networks Re-compete (NGEN-R) Service Management, Integration, and Transport (SMI&T) program.

2017

Leidos rises from No. 16 on a list of the largest government contractors to No. 1, with inorganic growth of 82 percent in one year.

already strong Leidos team. While Leidos remained headquartered in Reston, Virginia, the company would now also have an expanded presence through more than 400 locations.

Reagan said he knew after joining the company that Leidos and Krone were in the position to take large steps forward. "When I got here a couple of years ago, it was clear we had some pretty big plans and aspirations," Reagan said, and added:

> *Roger is not someone who is one for status quo. We had looked at a couple of opportunities, things that weren't quite the best fit, and then when the opportunity to partner up with the IS&GS business of Lockheed Martin came along, it became very interesting very quickly. ... The possibility for the future really is enabled by how well we've been integrating the IS&GS business so far, and by the time we're finished, we will be ready to take on another new challenge, and I'm sure that those opportunities will be coming along sometime in the near future.*

Krone and his management team decided early on in the acquisition process that it would not be treated as a takeover, but a merger. In any department where a Leidos person was picked to run an operation, the goal was to appoint an IS&GS person as a deputy, and vice versa.

Despite becoming a massive new company, Leidos also made it a goal to remain agile and adaptable. That occurred by keeping to a minimum the number of executives who reported directly to the CEO. And the number of management levels was kept at just four: the C-level executives, including presidents in civil, defense and intelligence, health, and advanced solutions; operation managers; division managers; and lastly the employees who report to those division managers. Such a short path upward meant employees at lower levels could retain the authority to make important decisions and keep the combined company nimble.

Above: Executive Vice President and Chief Financial Officer James Reagan.

Below: With the merger, Leidos became the industry's largest pure play IT services provider.

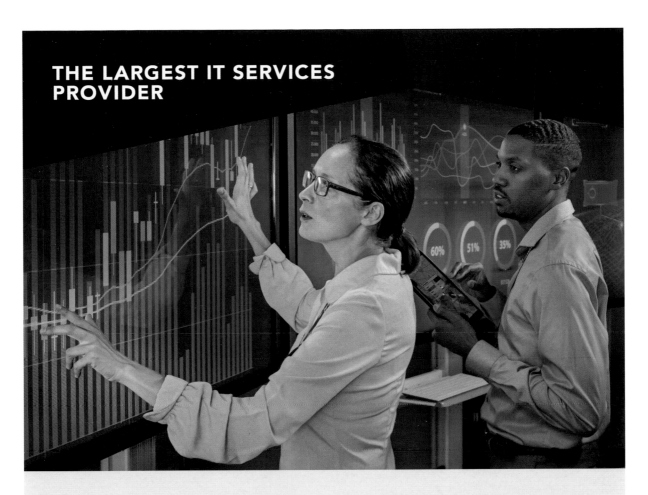

THE LARGEST IT SERVICES PROVIDER

As a result of the merger with the former Lockheed Martin IS&GS business, Leidos would become a leader in IT modernization, allowing the company to bid on contracts that it previously was not equipped to handle. Instead of working as a subcontractor, Leidos could now turn its attention toward large, multibillion-dollar enterprise IT contracts.

The IS&GS transaction created "a much more diversified set of core capabilities as well as a diversified customer base, which makes us a much stronger business that enables us to execute in a much more competitive environment," said Chief Financial Officer James Reagan at a May 2017 presentation. With the IS&GS business, "we are now the largest pure play IT services provider serving the U.S. federal government as well as government entities overseas."

In terms of the expanded capabilities that came as a result of combining with IS&GS, Ravi Hubbly, Leidos' vice president of data analytics, products, and services, who was with Lockheed Martin at the time of the merger, said:

We are providing very disruptive solutions that will be long lasting and stable compared to others. This is called our best-of-breed approach, which is what we bring to the table, rather than being a vendor that is very good at one thing. This approach works very well for our customer. I think that's our major differentiator.

The IS&GS transaction helped catapult the company to the top rankings of companies in its industry. In 2016, Leidos was ranked No. 16 on *Washington Technology*'s list of the largest government contractors. In 2017, after the merger, Leidos rose above Lockheed Martin to take the top spot, with $6.89 billion in contracts.

Bringing Highly Specialized Capabilities

With a large portfolio of projects, IS&GS brought with it existing contracts that would put Leidos in charge of advanced technological programs and operations. Among the largest was the $3 billion Hanford Mission Support project based at the Hanford Site, a decommissioned nuclear production complex in Washington State. The site got its start in 1943 as a plutonium production site for the Manhattan Project. Decades later, it is now one of the largest nuclear cleanup efforts in the world.

The $3 billion contract Leidos inherited from IS&GS with the Energy Department was to last 10 years. The project would help transition employees to mobile devices and virtual desktops. Through information management systems, the project also improved site operations for the Energy Department. IS&GS won the contract through a joint venture with Jacobs Technology and WSI. Leidos now provides sitewide services at Hanford, with integrated infrastructure aimed at moving the cleanup project forward.

Inset: As part of the merger, Leidos took over support operations at the Hanford site, among the largest nuclear cleanup projects in the world.

Below: Members of the Hanford Mission Support Alliance Information Management team discuss ways to prevent a data center outage.

Above: Systems
Engineer Kaitlyn
Ternay works at the
FAA's William J.
Hughes Technical
Center Virtual
Display Lab.

Below: Leidos
support in
Antarctica includes
remote field camps.
*(Photo courtesy of the
United States Antarctic
Program, National
Science Foundation
by photographer
Rachel Murray.)*

In combining with IS&GS, Leidos became the point company on projects to upgrade air traffic control systems with modern technology. Over the decades, IS&GS had been the lead company on billions of dollars of contracts with the Federal Aviation Administration (FAA). Systems in the Leidos portfolio would include En Route Automation Modernization (ERAM), Advanced Technologies & Oceanic Procedures (ATOP), Time Based Flow Management (TBFM), and Terminal Flight Data Manager (TFDM). Leidos would also provide SkyLine-X™ Air Traffic Management technology, which improves performance and increases fuel efficiency in countries including Albania, Kazakhstan, New Zealand, and South Korea. In the United Kingdom, the Leidos work with NATS (formerly the National Air Traffic Services) would also help upgrade the nation's air traffic control for the future through its deployment of the Single European Sky ATM Research (SESAR) program.

In 2011, Lockheed Martin won a $2 billion contract with the National Science Foundation's Antarctic Support Program, which began in 1956. Inheriting the project with the IS&GS transaction, Leidos took over the support and maintenance of infrastructure for the U.S. Antarctic Program. The project requires a different set of challenges for Leidos, working in perhaps the world's most remote and difficult terrains. The contract meant Leidos inherited the world's longest supply chain, which includes airfields etched into ice and snow. The work Leidos picked up allows researchers and universities from the United States and other

Above: Leidos inherited IS&GS's support operations for the U.S. mission in Antarctica.

Below: Angela Heise, president of the civil business at Leidos, briefs attendees at the Leidos Leadership Summit on January 24, 2018.

nations to conduct valuable scientific research. Most employees working on the contract arrive in Antarctica for the Southern Hemisphere's summer months, while a handful remain throughout the winter. They are stationed at field camps, three U.S. research facilities, and two research vessels.

Angela Heise, president of the company's civil business, was part of a team that traveled to Antarctica to oversee the Leidos logistic support services. She described how everyone on the frigid continent works together to help one another, no matter their country of origin:

> At our airfield, a Russian plane came in, they needed to refuel. We helped them, they refueled, and they went on their way. We had another instance where our team got diverted because of horrible weather coming back from the South Pole and they were welcomed at the Italian base with open arms, were fed, and given room until the weather cleared so they could get on their way. That entire continent operates that way. When you're flooded with news from around the world that's not necessarily positive, for me, that was absolutely inspirational.

Key Differentiators

The most specialized capabilities from IS&GS were in IT modernization, air traffic control, cybersecurity, biometrics, cloud computing, health, and data analytics. Among government contractors at the time, the combined company would be by far the largest pure play IT company in the United States "We now have the ability to pursue any program in any country in the world," Gerry Fasano, Leidos executive vice president and chief of Business Development & Strategy, said at the time. Fasano was with Lockheed Martin during the merger and managed the transition team with Leidos counterpart Mike Leiter.

After the merger, with the ability to bid on larger contracts than either company separately could take on, Leidos turned its sights on the potential of creating a modern version of the U.S. Navy's Next Generation Enterprise Networks Re-compete (NGEN-R) Service Management, Integration, and Transport (SMI&T) program. The contract was worth an estimated $3 billion to $5 billion. The contract for the Navy's next-generation system was up for re-compete, and the government was expected to select a new contractor in 2019.

The Navy's NGEN-R contract would cover a myriad of crucial tasks. It would enlarge government networks to increase design control and operations, with changing security requirements in mind. It would heighten the visibility of related costs and create more industry competition through cost efficiencies and innovation. The program would achieve this through integrating multiple enterprise networks into a common global network for the Department of Defense.

In February 2018, Leidos joined forces with several technology industry giants to bid on NGEN-R. The team included IBM, Unisys, and Verizon. After the announcement of the combined team, Krone said:

U.S. Navy Information Systems Technicians work together in 2013 to assess the security of the computer networks aboard the aircraft carrier USS *George H. W. Bush*. *(U.S. Navy photo by Mass Communication Specialist 2nd Class Leonard Adams Jr./ Released.)**

Leidos is a leading global solutions integrator with a prominent portfolio among the international federal IT solutions and service providers. The merger with Lockheed Martin's former Information Systems & Global Solutions business strengthened our scale to provide cost-effective, agile, and 'speed to mission' capabilities that solve our customers' most challenging problems. The Leidos team offers unmatched execution excellence, proven engineering rigor, and business analytics that can expertly support the Navy's critical missions anytime and anywhere.

After the merger, the company worked to avoid potential difficulties that could arise from weaving together different management styles, according to Frank Kendall, the former Under Secretary of Defense for Acquisition, Technology, and Logistics. Kendall now serves as a member of the Leidos Board of Directors and as executive in residence to aerospace and defense advisory firm Renaissance Strategic Advisors. "What you try to do in a merger like this is to take advantage of the strengths of both of the businesses and to try to overcome any weaknesses, and I think, in this case, that's what's been done," said Kendall, who added:

AWARDS AND RECOGNITION

Throughout its 50 years in business, Leidos has won scores of industry honors, including an Outstanding Prime Contractor Award from the Defense Contract Management Area Office of the Defense Logistics Agency for achievements in SAIC's Small Business Program. The company has also won the Department of Defense Patriot Award, a Champions of Veteran Enterprise Award, the Nunn-Perry Award, Space Flight Awareness Team Awards, and several others.

In 2018 alone, *Forbes* magazine added Leidos to its list of America's Best Employers in addition to the company being named to the magazine's Best Employers for Diversity list and as its Top 100 Corporate Citizens. Leidos was also was added to the Bloomberg Gender Equality Index, named a Top 100 Global Tech Leader by Thomson Reuters, a Best for Vets Employer by *Military Times, and* was honored with the James S. Cogswell Outstanding Industrial Security Achievement Award. In the healthcare arena, Leidos also achieved a Top 10 ranking on the Healthcare Informatics Top 100. The company also climbed into the Top 300 on the Fortune 500 list.

I think, to some degree, the former Lockheed part of Leidos has actually been more empowered and allowed to operate in a way that has been more successful within Leidos. And I also think that the technical strength of the Leidos/SAIC part of the company has been able to enhance the offerings of the Lockheed part. So there has been pluses on both sides. And I think that the way the management team at Leidos has handled the integration, and not having had either of the two major components be completely dominant over the other, basically made the integration much easier. It has made it much easier for people to feel comfortable and independent regardless of which part of the company they came from originally.

Employees work at the Leidos data center in Gaithersburg, Maryland.

Sondra L. Barbour, the former executive vice president of IS&GS from Lockheed Martin, was on the steering committee when the two organizations merged. "There were synergies there, from a people perspective, but by and large, it was the go-to-market capabilities that we felt were very complementary," Barbour said regarding the component she believed ultimately cemented the decision for the merger. Sharon Watts, former Leidos chief administrative officer, served as vice president of Engineering and Technology for IS&GS before the merger. "From technology, going to market, how we approach either customers, vendors, partners, or strategic partners, there's lots of similarities, and where there's differences, they turned out to be learning opportunities, not differences that provoke, if you will," Watts said.

Jerald S. "Jerry" Howe Jr. joined Leidos in July 2017 after working for the law firm Fried Frank, where he specialized in contract administration and mergers and acquisitions. His team was responsible for bringing the

Right: Jerry Howe, executive vice president and general counsel at Leidos, supported the merger of Lockheed Martin's IS&GS business with Leidos while at law firm Fried Frank.

Below: Leidos Chairman and CEO Roger Krone and Sondra L. Barbour, former executive vice president for IS&GS, speak to employees in a live webcast to Leidos offices during Day One celebration activities on August 16, 2016, in Reston, Virginia.

IS&GS contracts into Leidos, a complicated step due to the concentration of those contracts within the Lockheed Martin family. Howe recalled the intricacies involved in the transaction:

So the first thing we needed to do was to collect them all [the contracts] and then to bring them over as a totality to Leidos, and that in itself was a lot of work, but it also set up a process of approval by the government called novation, and novation is the way in which the government approves that transfer of contracts from one corporate family to another. And if you look at the government's own materials and announcements on the novation process, they typically say it's going to take 12, 15, 18 months, and by the way, don't bother us to try to accelerate that because it's generally going to be counterproductive for you to attempt to move it up. Well, that really wasn't something that we could accept as a business outcome, so we ended up getting it done in three and a half months.

Bringing International Strength

Before the merger with IS&GS, Leidos already had strong footholds in international markets. Among them were contracts with the U.S. Army to provide work at the Space and Missile Defense Command missile test ranges in Kwajalein Atoll in the Marshall Islands. But the 2016 transaction brought Leidos into several new markets and allowed the company to become a major contractor in others where it previously had a smaller presence.

The merger meant Leidos now had a major presence in the United Kingdom. But among the largest transitions was in Australia. There, 700 employees of Lockheed Martin Australia became Leidos, under the management of defense industry veteran Christine Zeitz. Previously, Leidos had 45 people working in Australia. Among the Australian contracts Leidos took over was the $943 million change program with the Australian Defence's Chief Information Officer Group. The new Leidos operation in Australia also handled IT for several agencies, including the Australian Tax Office, a contract worth about $60 million a year.

Expanding the Leidos reach into new international markets could have created management dilemmas for many companies. But even though the merger created the largest corporation in the industry, the newly formed company had less bureaucracy, said Ann Addison, former Leidos executive vice president and chief human resources officer. "Actually, Lockheed Martin [IS&GS] wanted less bureaucracy, and you found that Leidos wanted a little

With 20 years of experience, Leidos Australia now employs more than 1,000 people.

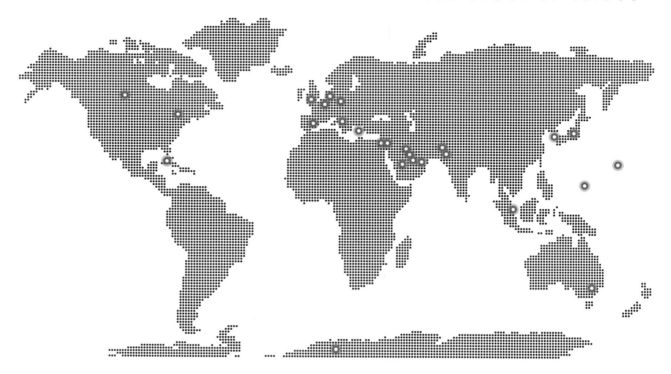

Above: With more than 400 locations in 30 countries, Leidos is dedicated to becoming the global leader in the integration and application of information technology.

Below: Ann Addison, former chief human resources officer for Leidos.

bit more structure. You found that Lockheed Martin [IS&GS] wanted maybe less rigidity in decision making, and maybe Leidos wanted a little bit more structure on how they did decision making. So the aspirational culture actually was pretty close," Addison said. To assure the two organizations could come together, the Executive Leadership Team worked with a consultant and sent a survey out to all Leidos employees. Executives also took the survey and participated in one-on-one discussions on what they would like the new company's management to look like. Addison added:

> *We really wanted to keep all the structure and the process efficiency from the Lockheed Martin [IS&GS] side, but the [Leidos] innovation and passion to win, and being able to reinvest back into the organizations that are winning, we wanted to take both of those cultures and go forward and create an absolutely winning culture that took the best of both and was even stronger.*

Building Opportunities for Customers

Most importantly, the merger allowed Leidos to better serve its customers. "The combined company will be more diversified and have more customer touch points between civil, defense, and intelligence, and we will be able to leverage our learnings across this broad set to offer even more innovative solutions at an even faster clip to our customers, enabling them to meet their mission needs likely sooner, more elegantly, and at lower cost than they would have otherwise," a company statement said about the merger.

The merger also allowed cuts to redundant overhead costs from both Leidos and IS&GS divisions. In 2016, Leidos hoped to cut $25 million in redundant costs, and the company hit that number by the third quarter, two months ahead of schedule. Analysts responded by giving Leidos favorable marks for its work after the merger, with Credit Suisse upgrading the Leidos stock from "neutral" to "outperform."

Subsequent to the merger, the company decided the customer would be best served if the new enterprise didn't adopt all of the procedures from Leidos or IS&GS. Instead, the newly joined entities would analyze the differences between the two companies and pick the better procedures, whether they originated at Lockheed Martin or Leidos. At the time, Watts described some of the methodological differences between the two companies:

Vicki Schmanske followed Sharon Watts as Leidos chief administrative officer in 2018. Schmanske previously served as deputy president and chief operations officer for the company's health business and as vice president of operations for IS&GS.

> *Where we really see the difference in the two cultures is that heritage Leidos has more of a scientific think tank kind of thought process, where I would say IS&GS may be more command and control. Leidos is more of a turn on a dime and go. IS&GS has always been more methodical, thinking through things. It's not a slower process to get to the same place, but it's just very different how the same conclusion comes out, even though the pace between Leidos and IS&GS is different. I think that's been, for me personally, the biggest challenge of blending the two cultures—the different pace of business coming from each side. It's amazing when you slow down a bit what you can learn, and what can be learned on the command and control end of the spectrum.*

While the heritage and methodologies between the two companies were different, one major reason the merger was so seamless came as a result of the dedicated work ethic from both the IS&GS and the Leidos sides. "It's going be an ongoing effort for some time, and the people are already working together, side-by-side," said Melissa Koskovich, Leidos senior vice president and director of Communications and Marketing, who added:

> *I think there's definitely common values between Leidos and IS&GS. The passion that people have for working for the customers, the commitment, definitely value integrity, it's kind of the core for everything that everyone does, and just ultimately, people wanting to do meaningful work. The people who walk through these doors every day, this is their life's work, and they want to contribute in some way. … I think we share those values across both sides.*

After spending 19 years at Lockheed Martin, Heise said her initial reaction when learning about the possible merger was concern. "It really took a little time for me to try to get my head wrapped around what that might mean for me personally and professionally," Heise said. "But I will tell you, Day One, August 16 of 2016, I will never forget because it exceeded expectations for me in every single way, because I felt absolutely welcome. I felt I had a voice that was valued and that, all of a sudden, as a person who started off as a software

Employees watch a video presentation during Day One celebration activities on August 16, 2016 in Reston, Virginia, following the merger of Lockheed Martin's IS&GS group with Leidos.

engineer 20 years ago, I was in a company where our entire workforce resonates with software engineering and IT and science. That is a core value of this corporation and one of the reasons that I've spent the last year really excited and optimistic about the future of our company."

In February 2018, the company's reported revenue in the final quarter of 2017 hit $2.52 billion, up 2.3 percent from the prior year. That helped revenues for 2017 reach $10.17 billion, compared to $7.04 billion the prior year. The 44.4 percent increase occurred as the company orchestrated perhaps the largest merger in the industry's history. "We closed out 2017 with another strong quarter of operational performance, enabling us to achieve strong margins and generate more than half a billion dollars of cash from operations for the year," Krone said and added:

> With the successful completion of most of our integration activities, we shift our focus to growth in the year ahead. Our strong balance sheet and increased cash generation allows us to continue to invest for growth while also returning capital to shareholders. Further, the talent and diversity of our employees, combined with their dedication to delivering mission-critical solutions, gives us confidence in our ability to deliver value to our customers and shareholders.

The successful merger shows Leidos can take on large challenges and come out stronger, demonstrating its ability to successfully integrate and build growth back into the company. ∎

Krone made closing remarks at the 2017 Leidos Leadership Summit on January 31, 2017.

Scanning....

010010011100111100111100110111
111100110010100110010010010010
0001100011000110010101

CHAPTER TWELVE

INVENTING THE FUTURE

It has been a pretty interesting and rewarding journey. We've now doubled the size of the company, we're performing really well in our programs, and I think we've made it a great place to come to work. We're building the Leidos brand, and we're really building it through performance.

─────────────

Roger Krone
CHAIRMAN AND CEO

L OOKING BACK TO 1969, J. ROBERT BEYSTER STARTED THE FIRM WITH the simple vision of helping others through scientific discoveries. It's clear that Leidos has not only met that goal but also shows no signs of slowing down. Leidos has taken the lessons and achievements from the last 50 years and has used them to fuel its mission to make the world safer, healthier, and more efficient through its 31,000 global employees who have an unrelenting passion for delivering innovative solutions to solve their customers' most demanding challenges.

As it has for the past five decades, Leidos is a company continually looking forward. But inventing the future is a challenging prospect with the staggering advance of technology. All around the world, technology is becoming more complex and more intertwined with nearly every aspect of human life. The needs of Leidos' customers are also changing, demanding new solutions in IT modernization, cybersecurity, and artificial intelligence (AI). The company cannot achieve its mission using only the technologies and solutions available today. As the challenges accelerate, the solutions must keep pace. Thankfully, the advance of technology is also providing the solutions to its own challenges. Leidos Chairman and CEO Roger Krone addressed this future in a 2018 speech to the Atlantic Council, a U.S.-based international affairs think tank:

Opposite: The future of Leidos is one filled with endless possibilities, as the company's work in some of the most advanced areas of science and technology will continue to expand to create critical solutions that change the world. *(Photo courtesy of iStock.com/zmeel.)*

A visionary leader: Chairman and CEO Roger Krone speaking to the Atlantic Council as part of its 2018 Captains of Industry series.

We live in an uncertain and evolving world that is becoming more digital and more connected at ever-increasing speeds. ... The evolution in technology is having a major impact on our customers, who are feeling the pressure to modernize, drive ever-increasing efficiencies, and secure their aging IT environments from an emerging virtual threat. Moore's law, Metcalf's law, the cost of storage and the move to virtualization are all pacing a rate of change in our world that even most large organizations are challenged to keep up.

As a result, what customers want from companies like Leidos is changing. Services are not enough. It's not just labor as an extension of the customer. Our industry is changing to highly skilled labor, solving customer problems, and supporting customer mission.

2010

Leidos sets a goal of reducing greenhouse gasses 25 percent by 2020.

2014

Six years before the company's goal, Leidos hits targets of reducing greenhouse gasses by 25 percent.

2015

Leidos secures its first major support deal with the U.K. Defence Ministry to transform how military commodities are procured and stored.

2015

Leidos employees put in 16,732 hours through the year as volunteers on company-directed community relations activities.

An Innovation Edge in an Evolving Marketplace

Innovation has been critical to the company's success in supporting its customers' success. Leidos intentionally cultivates an environment where every solution delivered to the customer is affected by its 50-year culture of innovation.

At Leidos, the idea is more than a nebulous concept. The company defines innovation as "the implementation of new ideas with business impact." This definition means that innovation happens not just within technology research and development and customer programs, but perhaps within its accounting department, its procurement processes, or within its contracting terms.

The Leidos definition of innovation also demands an approach that includes a level of practicality to the company's efforts. Employees are not dealing simply in the theoretical, but also in the application of those

Leidos biology laboratory facilities in San Diego enable advanced research and development for a variety of U.S. government customers. *(Photo courtesy of James Aronovsky.)*

2016

For the second year in a row, Leidos logs $2 million in charitable contributions. That tally would double the following year as a result of the merger with Lockheed Martin's former IS&GS business.

2016

Through years of conservation efforts by employees, Leidos sees dramatic drops in water consumption, electrical use, and transportation costs. Meanwhile, the company increases its recycling and composting efforts.

2016

Leidos employees put in 18,218 hours through the year as volunteers on company-directed community relations activities.

2017

CREDIT: PHOTO BY ZAID HAMID.

Chairman and CEO Roger Krone receives an e-mail from employee John Hindman (pictured), leading Krone and Leidos to take an active role in fighting the growing opioid epidemic.

theories and ideas. While Leidos scientists, engineers, and technologists certainly look five, ten, fifteen years out, employees are also skilled enough to know how to get there, and how to apply the iterative technologies to customer needs—making an impact. Employees believe their ideas and solutions have to be attainable to be transformative. This crawl, walk, run philosophy ensures that progress continues and innovation is tangibly achieved.

Leidos fosters innovation particularly in areas that leverage its core technical capabilities, viewing technology innovation as a symbiotic relationship between internal and customer-related R&D efforts. If Leidos is working on advancing its core technical competencies related to future market opportunities, the company uses its internal R&D. When a solution is tied to a specific customer need, Leidos aggressively pursues that business development opportunity through RFPs or contracts to directly convert R&D into business profit and then extend the solution across its customer portfolio. The company's strong track record at the service and research labs, DARPA, and IARPA reflect this innovation philosophy.

Leidos is uniquely situated at the intersection of the federal, commercial, and academic environments to scan the technology horizon and rapidly bring it to bear for its customers. The company is able to watch for signs of change in markets, assess their potential effects, and apply or create the right technologies to benefit its customers' missions.

One area where this will be increasingly true is the area of cybersecurity. While Leidos works on a myriad of current cybersecurity efforts, the company is also imagining what cybersecurity and related attacks will look like in the near and distant future. Leidos is ready across multiple government and industry markets with staff who are trained specifically in this

2017

Leidos employees put in 25,500 hours through the year as volunteers on company-directed community relations activities.

2017

Efforts to expand overseas have resulted in 9 percent of the company's business occurring outside the United States.

2017

Leidos Australia opens a high-tech collaboration space, known as CONNECT, in Canberra to showcase its capabilities and technology partners.

2017

Leidos inks a deal for a new headquarters at 1750 Presidents Street in Reston Town Center. The 267,000 square-foot, 17-story building will house 1,000 Leidos employees.

area, with continuous monitoring and regular incident response reviews to incorporate what has been learned from previous attacks.

For the Department of Defense, Leidos is helping to protect against cybersecurity attacks with strategy and planning that can prevent an attack before it occurs. Predictive analytics applied to network data protection can more quickly review information that must be assessed from a variety of data streams and devices. Machine speeds have progressed fast enough that analytical math can now handle computations that previously had only been theoretical. The systems allow human security operators to make better decisions sooner on how to react to cyberattacks. Today, Leidos is

With cyber security an ever-increasing concern, Leidos' position at the intersection of federal, commercial, and academic environments enables it to rapidly bring cutting-edge solutions to its customers.

2017   **2017**   **2018**   **2018**

Leidos' dominance in the IT field is recognized by the National Geospatial-Intelligence Agency, which awards the company a contract worth $988 million.

CR Magazine's Responsible CEO of the Year is Leidos CEO Roger Krone, recognized for the company's high standards in areas including human rights and corporate responsibility.

Second quarter net bookings total $3.4 billion, including work for the U.S. Department of Energy, the Department of Veterans Affairs Administration, and members of the intelligence community, setting the company up for continued success into the future.

Matt Wiles (left), who served as air secretary while in the Royal Air Force and joined Leidos U.K. in April 2016, is named the new Leidos U.K. CEO.

working with the Department of Defense on self-learning and self-healing networks that can "make networks more resilient in the face of an attack," said Keith Johnson, chief technology officer and chief engineer.

In the healthcare field, Leidos is seeing a trend in companies that want to outsource application modernization, data center consolidation, and seat management. "Technology advancements present a host of opportunities for hospital systems to improve efficiencies that ultimately drive better health outcomes," said William Kloes, president of commercial health at Leidos, who added:

> *Leidos partners with organizations on priority modernization and optimization areas so that hospital systems can focus on their primary mission: providing wellness and care to the populations they serve. Phenomenal advancements in care delivery are executed at our client sites every day. We ensure that the enterprise IT environment keeps pace with their advancing needs, absorbing burdensome aspects of their IT operations so they can focus their investments and strategy on the business of healthcare.*

A Growing International Presence

Historically, international operations represented a small portion of Leidos' revenues. That began to change in 2015, when the company set its sights on expanding overseas. In 2017, 9 percent of Leidos' revenues came from international business. The United Kingdom and Europe together represent the company's largest international presence. The 1,500 employees there work with the Ministry of Defence, Ministry of Justice, NATS, NATO, and other agencies.

In Europe and the U.K., Leidos teams work on improving defense supply chains, modernization of IT systems, a full spectrum of cybersecurity services, airport security, air traffic control, data analytics, and clinical and technical expertise in the health field. In Scotland alone, projects include a procurement directorate with the Scottish government and ScottishPower's innovation in process safety.

Leidos secured its first major support deal with the U.K. Ministry of Defence in 2015. The multi billion-dollar program is aimed at transforming how military commodities are procured and stored. At the outset, the procurement items include clothing, food, fuel, and other items. The work is conducted through 70 warehouses across 11 sites. Officially known as the Logistic Commodities and Services Transformation (LCST) program, the project is expected to last 13 years and is worth as much as $12.2 billion.

In January 2018, the U.K. unit of Leidos received a new leader. Matt Wiles, formerly a senior vice president and managing director, became the company's

A CULTURE OF GIVING BACK

Leidos has long been committed to serving the communities where it operates. In both 2015 and 2016, the company logged $2 million in charitable giving each year. In 2015, Leidos employees put in 16,732 hours as volunteers, and in 2016 they topped that number by reaching 18,218 hours in volunteering. After the addition of the former IS&GS employees, the total hours donated reached 25,500 in 2017.

CR Magazine recognized Leidos' community efforts in October 2017 by naming CEO Roger Krone as Responsible CEO of the Year for exceeding "standards in the areas of employee relations, environmental impact, sustainability, human rights, philanthropy, and corporate responsibility practices."

CR Board CEO Dave Armon presented the award to Krone and stated:

One of the hardest parts of a CEO's job is management of culture. [Roger] had to rebuild one. Leidos was formed from the separation of its business from its predecessor, SAIC. Roger Krone joined just after this separation and began the process of helping reshape the company's vision of itself. He recognized the importance of community engagement and began an effort to set aside a significant percentage of pre-tax profits for philanthropy.

Above: U.K. Chief Executive Matt Wiles (left) accepts an Excellence in Collaboration award on behalf of Michelle Raven from Chairman and CEO Roger Krone (right) during the 2017 Achievement Awards Ceremony at the 2018 Leidos Leadership Summit.

Right: Leidos Australia employees in the Canberra-based NCITE facility.

new U.K. chief executive. Wiles joined Leidos U.K. in April 2016 and, as part of his duties, oversaw the LCST program with the U.K. defense ministry. While in the Royal Air Force, Wiles served as air secretary, chief of staff personnel, and director of the joint support chain at the U.K. defense ministry. "I am delighted to have been appointed Chief Executive of Leidos U.K. at such an exciting time for our clients' challenges and opportunities as well as for our business," said Wiles. "The success of our work with the MoD, across the British Government to organisations that are critical to our national infrastructure, such as NATS, shows that we are a trusted partner in the U.K. and that our people can deliver innovative solutions to solve the most complex problems."

Before the merger, both Leidos and IS&GS operated facilities in Australia. After the companies merged, their presence in Australia represented a sizable portion of Leidos' international operations. That continued to expand in 2017. Leidos Australia opened Leidos CONNECT in Canberra. The high-tech collaboration space showcases capabilities and technology partners, such as Cisco and Microsoft, in one space. "We've committed to investing $12 million over the next seven years," said Christine Zeitz, Leidos Australia chief executive. "This gives our customers and partners a place to workshop their challenges and develop innovative new solutions."

Also in Australia in 2017, Leidos signed a five-year sponsorship with the Bravery Trust. Veterans of the Australian Defence Force and their families receive urgent financial support through the organization. Since its founding in 2012, the Bravery Trust has helped more than 2,200 veterans and their families. Zeitz said Leidos Australia's team of more than 1,000 people matches well with the Bravery Trust, as the two organizations are both seeing growth and share many synergies. Bravery Trust CEO Sean Farrell agreed. "Leidos Australia is Bravery Trust's major industry partner, and we are thrilled to have them on board," said Farrell. "While they are focused on supporting the business of defense and government, we are focused on supporting veterans and their families. I think we have a great match here and I look forward to working with the Leidos Australia team."

Driven by Excellence

As the CEO of Leidos, Krone believes every leader must plan for the future. At Leidos, he has found that those plans are dependent on a framework that was developed following the integration of the IS&GS business. The company's strategy includes executing on its commitments, differentiating itself from competitors, growing the business, and energizing its talented team. Krone believes the key to the company's success in the future is simply continuing to execute on this strategy. "It's kind of what I do. I've got to get the mission, vision, and strategy of the company right," said Krone. "We're just in a better place, because unlike some of the smaller

Krone joined in the Day One fun by handing out ice cream during celebration activities after combining with Lockheed Martin's former IS&GS business unit.

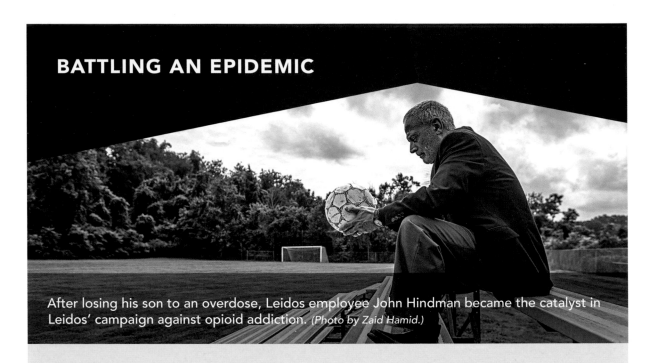

BATTLING AN EPIDEMIC

After losing his son to an overdose, Leidos employee John Hindman became the catalyst in Leidos' campaign against opioid addiction. (*Photo by Zaid Hamid.*)

While Leidos has always supported several charitable causes, there was one cause that became personal to the company and CEO Roger Krone after an employee challenged him to bring more attention to this particular issue. That issue is the growing epidemic of opioid addiction. "This individual had lost his son, so he's an employee coming to the CEO asking, 'Is there anything you can do about this? It's clearly a major epidemic-level challenge for the nation and the world,'" said Michael Coogan, Leidos' director of corporate responsibility, who added:

Roger became very passionate about opioid addiction, and the subject really started to gain steam in mid- to late 2017, so we stepped back and asked ourselves, "What can we do internally for our employees and externally, both about awareness and taking it on as a company challenge?" That's what we're about, is solving problems, not just for our customers' major challenges, but what can we do about these major societal issues? It started with an individual employee,

companies, we don't need to do another transaction. We can pick and choose and look at a transaction that furthers the strategic interest of the corporation."

Leidos Chief Financial Officer James Reagan, who started with Leidos in 2015, said of the company's strategy for success:

We will never be done growing. We will never be done finding new ways to leverage the capability of this great enterprise to more customers and finding new things to bring to the customers that we already have. I think the most important thing for us to do is to grow faster than our competitors and to add value. When our investors, when all of our stakeholders, can see that we can

and then it became very apparent to us that a company our size with roughly 31,000 employees, whether directly or indirectly—we're being impacted by this issue.

According to the Centers for Disease Control, the opioid epidemic costs the United States approximately $500 billion each year. And given the fact that more Americans have died from drug overdoses in one year than the number of U.S. soldiers who were lost in Vietnam, Desert Storm, Desert Shield, and Enduring Freedom—combined, the problem became a compelling reason for Leidos to boldly take action. The company did just that, by raising awareness, providing assistance to struggling employees or family members, sponsoring charitable programs, and partnering with academia to ensure that the right messaging about the issue is communicated to students.

Krone became so passionate about fighting opioid addiction that he would often bring up the topic at speaking engagements, including during a speech he gave to the Atlantic Council in April 2018, where he stated:

We must all get involved in order to provoke behavioral change. So today—I want to use this forum to challenge all of us to think about how we can use our collective brain power, entrepreneurship, innovation, and influence to present new ideas, policy, and technology that can make a difference in this fight against the opioid epidemic.

Today, Leidos is working with several nonprofit partners to combat opioid addiction and the stigma associated with it. Two of the company's partners working on this initiative are the Chris Atwood Foundation, which is focused on recovery, and the Community Anti-Drug Coalitions of America (CADCA), which is focused on awareness and prevention. Leidos also continues to encourage other large corporations and their leadership to join them in the fight to make opioid addiction a thing of the past, as Krone stated:

… industry yields considerable strength in doing something about this issue, as it's our collective responsibility to serve our communities.

use our competitive advantage to do better than our peers, do better than our competitors, we'll find ourselves gaining share and growing the business at a faster clip than the industry. This is how you build shareholder value, through deep customer relationships with the ability to put the customer first and do the right thing for the customer. When you're doing the right thing for the customer, you're doing the right thing for the employees, you're doing the right thing for shareholders, and that's how you build long-term shareholder value.

When it comes to where Leidos as a company will be in the next few years, its continued success also depends on Leidos employees' expertise, their drive to make a difference, and their commitment to collaborate with their

Opposite: Executive Vice President and Chief Financial Officer for Leidos, James Reagan, speaking at the Leidos Leadership Summit, January 26, 2016, at the Reston Hyatt regarding the merger between Leidos and Lockheed Martin's IS&GS Business.

COMMITMENT TO THE PLANET

Leidos has a strong commitment to the planet, and in 2010, the company created a goal to cut its greenhouse gas emissions by 25 percent by 2020. In 2014, Leidos achieved the goal six years ahead of schedule. By 2015, the company cut these emissions by another 22 percent. Greenhouse gasses were reduced through real estate restructuring and improved efficiency programs executed by employees. Increased use of renewable energy in Leidos facilities helped facilitate that greenhouse gas emission drop and helped make the company more efficient.

In 2016, the company composted 31,104 pounds and recycled 1.18 million pounds. Electricity consumption by the company dropped every year for the past six years; in 2016, the company used 83,417-megawatt hours of electricity, down from 206,319-megawatt hours in 2011. Water consumption by the company has also dropped every year for the past six years, from 69,915 kilogallons in 2011 to 17,331 kilogallons in 2016. In San Diego, for instance, the campus uses reclaimed water to irrigate the landscaping in an effort to preserve the city's drinking water.

In addition, by promoting flex work, Leidos has reduced the company's environmental impact and also reduced the negative effects of employee travel. From 2011 to 2016, Leidos reduced its car rentals from 55,041 to 39,512 and its domestic and international airline trips from 109,568 to 43,247 in the effort to do its part for the environment.

Unleash Your Inner Purple

colleagues and the customer. Regarding recruitment of more talented employees for the Leidos team, Jim Cantor, Leidos chief engineering executive, added:

> *I would say what Leidos can offer somebody coming in is the opportunity to work with people who are really passionate about a mission, and I think that's been the cornerstone of SAIC that kind of grew in Leidos, and undoubtedly it's true of our new brethren from IS&GS. A lot of reasons why people would want to work here and not necessarily maybe in a commercial area is because they see a larger purpose, a larger opportunity to effect positive change, and to grow.*

While recruitment has always played an important role in the success of Leidos, the company will continue to build on all of its strengths as it grows. "Over the next two to three years, how we're going to deliver value is pretty simple: use the Leidos platform, great people, strong capabilities, and a diverse customer set to drive revenue growth," Reagan said.

Regarding the company's accomplishments throughout its history, Krone said:

> *Reaching 50 years is a significant achievement for a company. But beyond the years themselves, the impact that Leidos has made for our customers and their missions will be the lasting testament of this great company. Over 50 years, tens of thousands of employees have dedicated their careers to the advancement of information technology, engineering, and science here at Leidos. I believe their efforts have combined to make our world safer, healthier, and more efficient, and I hope to see the company continue doing that same work long into the future.* ∎

Above: As part of the new branding in 2013, Leidos adopts purple as its main corporate color, which reflects the uniqueness of Leidos' diverse capabilities.

Below: Krone, like everyone at Leidos, looks forward to developing scientific and technological solutions to solve tomorrow's critical challenges.

REMEMBERING J. ROBERT BEYSTER

In 2014, company founder J. Robert Beyster, 90, passed away. Beyster was remembered as "a brilliant scientist and an equally brilliant businessman" who among many contributions to the world, saw the Internet's potential "when most were still skeptics," said retired U.S. Marine Major General Arnold Punaro. After graduating from the University of Michigan with a doctorate in physics, Beyster began his professional career at Westinghouse's Atomic Power Division, and in 1957, he took a job at General Atomics as the chairman of the Accelerator Physics Department. In 1969, after General Atomics was sold, Beyster would go on to found Science Applications International (SAI), using the proceeds from the sale of his company stock to fund his startup, and he never looked back.

Remembered as much as a brilliant businessman as for his ground-breaking contributions to science and technology, Beyster was also passionate about giving back to the business community. He founded two nonprofit groups, the Beyster Institute and the Foundation for Enterprise Development that both teach business owners about the concept of employee ownership, which Beyster championed and wrote about in his book *The SAIC Solution: How We Built an $8 Billion Employee-Owned Technology Company*.

In 2011, Beyster told *Washington Technology*:

> My vision was simply to create a good place for people—the company's engineers and scientists—to work. I also wanted the company to have a strong culture of entrepreneurship where people would be free to identify and pursue new business opportunities and then be rewarded for their successes.

Among his philanthropic work, Beyster and his wife, Betty Jean Beyster, donated $15 million to the University of Michigan's College of Engineering to support entrepreneurship programs. The couple also donated $8 million to build the University of San Diego's new nursing center.

Mark Sopp, former chief financial officer of SAIC, said of Beyster's legacy: "There are still many people here who personally knew Bob and had worked with him, and so he has never—and will never—be forgotten in the company. There's a piece of Bob Beyster in both SAIC and Leidos many years later that is still an important part of the mission, the culture, and the history." ∎

BIBLIOGRAPHY

BOOKS AND ARTICLES

44 Years of Success: A Timeline of Our History and Legacy, SAIC internal book, 2013.

"5 Corporations Now Dominate Our Privatized Intelligence Industry," *The Nation*, 8 September 2016.

"Analyst: Leidos 'fast becoming the most interesting story' in government services sector," *Washington Business Journal*, 21 November 2016.

Bartlett, Donald L. and Steele, James B., "Washington's $8 Billion Shadow," *Vanity Fair*, 6 February 2007.

Behr, Peter, "Just Say Know," *The Washington Post*, 1 April 1996.

"Beyond meaningful use: How enterprise IT modernization enables providers to focus on improving outcomes," *Healthcare IT News*, 25 February 2018.

Beyster, J. Robert and Economy, Peter, *The SAIC Solution: Built by Employee Owners*, copyright 2007 and 2014, The Foundation for Enterprise Development, La Jolla, California.

"Black founder of Internet domain registry, Network Solutions, reminisces on racial barriers in tech sector," *The Grio*, 28 June 2012.

Black, Norman, "Pentagon Selects Two More Contractor Teams for Missile Defense Project," Associated Press, 15 August 1985.

Borak, Donna, "Pentagon's Latest Probe: Fido's Nose," Associated Press, 3 October 2008.

Burns, Stan, *SAIC: The First Thirty Years*, Tehabi Books, Del Mar, California, copyright 1999, Science Applications International Corporation.

"California And The West; Science Applications Files Plan for IPO," *Los Angeles Times*, 2 September 2005.

Coker, Margaret, "Terrorism Fears Drive Games Security Plan," *The Atlanta Journal-Constitution*, 1 February 2004.

"Department of Defense Releases – Contracts," Defense Department Documents and Publications, 16 November 2016.

"Enhancing airport resilience and runway capacity – an Intelligent Approach," NATS Customer Affairs, 14 September 2017.

"Exclusive: John Jumper explains why the Leidos-SAIC split had to happen," *Washington Business Journal*, 26 September 2013.

"Following SAIC split, John Jumper to depart," *The Washington Post*, 19 February 2014.

"For the Record," *The Washington Post*, 21 July 1989.

"Gartner: 10 Fastest Growing Cybersecurity Consulting Companies," *CRN*, 22 August 2017.

Geer, Carolyn T., "Turning Employees Into Stakeholders," *Forbes*, 1 December 1997.

"Georgia Tech Names Engineering Biosystems Building for Krone Family," *Georgia Tech News Center*, 24 October 2017.

"Greece ordered to pay SAIC more than $52 million for breach of contract," *Washington Business Journal*, 18 July 2013.

Grover, Ronald, "Secretive SAIC Goes Public," *Bloomberg*, 6 September 2005.

Hagland, Mark, "Most Interesting Vendors 2016: Leidos: Healthcare IT's 'Quiet Company' Becoming Less Quiet By the Day," *Healthcare Informatics*, 23 May 2016.

Hansen, Matthew, "Supercomputer Lures Defense Lab The Kiewit Institute Expects to Announce Several More Partnerships in the Next Week," *Omaha World-Herald*, Nebraska, 1 August 2007.

Henderson, Nell, "Airlines Must Check for Plastic Bombs at 40 International Airports," *The Washington Post*, 31 August 1989.

"Homeland Security Goes Public," *Forbes*, 3 August 2006.

"How data, analytics and context help secure DoD systems," *Federal News Radio*, 14 November 2017.

"How do you split a multibillion dollar company? Ask Pamplin MBA alumnus Doug Wagoner," *Virginia Tech News*, 5 November 2013.

"Inside SAIC's pending divorce," *Washington Technology*, 19 June 2013.

"IPO catapults SAIC into a new era," *Washington Technology*, 12 May 2007.

Ivory, Danielle, "J. Robert Beyster, Scientist and Entrepreneur, Is Dead at 90," *The New York Times*, 23 December 2014.

Jayakumar, Amrita, "One Year Later: The Tale of SAIC and Leidos," *The Washington Post*, 28 September 2014.

"J. Robert Beyster dies at 90; founder of defense giant SAIC," *Los Angeles Times*, 23 December 2014.

"J. Robert Beyster, Who Founded Defense Contracting Giant SAIC, Dies at 90," *The Washington Post*, 1 January 2015.

"John Jumper to retire as Leidos CEO, five months after leading the corporate split of SAIC," *Washington Business Journal*, 19 February 2014.

Landi, Heather, "VA Awards Leidos $29 Million Health Data Contract," *Healthcare Informatics*, 18 April 2017.

"Leidos Australia opens tech collaboration facility in Canberra," *ARN*, 1 December 2017.

"Leidos captivates with unique new website and takes home a Bulldog Award," *Bulldog Reporter*, 20 May 2015.

"Leidos Demos New Unmanned Surface Vessel Technologies," *Unmanned Systems Technology*, 22 August 2017.

"Leidos forms CBRN partnership with University of New South Wales," *Jane's Defence Weekly*, 29 November 2017.

"Leidos has Navy NGEN contract 'in our pipeline,'" *Washington Technology*, 14 June 2017.

"Leidos Operates Night Eagle in Afghanistan," *Signal Magazine*, 23 September 2015.

"Leidos reports 44.4% revenue surge in FY17," *Geospatial World*, 23 February 2018.

"Leidos secures $777 million contract with Army Geospatial Center," *Fed Scoop*, 20 September 2016.

"Leidos takes top spot on 2017 Top 100," *Washington Technology*, 6 June 2017.

"Leidos Triumphs in Major UK Support Bid," *Defense News*, 18 February 2015.

"Leidos wins $662M award to upgrade Army reconnaissance aircraft fleet," *Washington Business Journal*, 6 November 2015.

"Leidos Wins Massive Pentagon Health Care Records Contract," *Nextgov*, 29 July 2015.

"Leidos' future CEO Roger Krone on leading a 'new old company,'" *Washington Business Journal*, 1 July 2014.

"Lockheed Martin IS&GS becomes Leidos," *Australian Defence Magazine*, 19 August 2016.

"Lockheed to Pair IS&GS Business with Leidos," *Defense News*, 26 January 2016.

"Long owned by employees, SAIC says it's going public," *The San Diego Union-Tribune*, 2 September 2005.

"Managing change to meet market challenges: A NATS case study," Business Case Studies, 2017.

Millard, Mike, "SAIC Acquires maxIT Healthcare for $473M," *Healthcare IT News*, 18 July 2012.

"Network Solutions Shares Surge 30 Percent in IPO," *The Washington Post*, 27 September 1997.

"No. 5: IPO Catapults SAIC Into a New Era," *Washington Technology*, 12 May 2007.

"One year later: The tale of SAIC and Leidos," *The Washington Post*, 28 September 2014.

Reagan, James, Leidos CFO, "Oppenheimer 12th Annual Industrial Growth Conference" presentation, 9 May 2017.

"Research Analysts' Recent Ratings Changes for Leidos (LDOS)," *Stock News Times*, 7 March 2018.

"SAIC founder chronicles past success," *San Diego Community News Group*, 17 August 2007.

"SAIC Founder J. Robert Beyster Dies," *The San Diego Union-Tribune*, 22 December 2014.

"SAIC Offering Raises $1 Billion," *The Washington Post*, 14 October 2006.

"SAIC Officially Moves Headquarters to Washington Area," *The San Diego Tribune*, 24 September 2009.

"SAIC Reaches Agreement With Greece," Associated Press, 4 April 2007.

"SAIC says IPO to raise more than $1.1 billion," *The San Diego Union-Tribune*, 3 October 2006.

"SAIC stock up 21% on 1st day," *Huntsville Times*, 14 October 2006.

"SAIC to support U.S. Darpa's ACTUV programme," *Naval Technology*, 19 August 2012.

"Senate Appropriations Subcommittee on Defense Hearing," Congressional Documents and Publications, 29 March 2017.

"Shareholders OK SAIC plan to restructure," Knight-Ridder Tribune Business News, 28 September 2006.

"Simulator provides safe, cost effective training alternative," *The Fort Campbell Courier*, 14 March 2013.

"Students crowned UK's most talented in cyber-security," *SC Media*, 20 March 2017.

"The 50 best companies to work for in America," *Business Insider*, 27 April 2015.

"Trading of SAIC stock begins today; shares are set at $15; IPO price is buoyed by interest, Dow surge," *The San Diego Union-Tribune*, 13 October 2006.

"U.S. Army Could Pay Leidos $64M for Reconnaissance Systems," *Avionics*, 18 July 2017.

"U.S. Army orders additional Saturn Arch aerial anti-IED platform," *Air Recognition*, 19 May 2017.

"Virginia Security Firm Hired to Develop Plan for WTC Site," Associated Press, 10 November 2005.

Wakeman, Nick, "Inside SAIC's $500M Health IT Acquisition," *Washington Technology*, 26 July 2012.

"Washington's $8 Billion Shadow," *Vanity Fair*, 6 February 2007.

"What's Leidos Getting for $5B?" *FCW*, 28 January 2016.

Whittman, Robert L., Jr., "OneSAF: A Product Line Approach to Simulation Development," Mitre Corporation, 2001.

"With help of branding agency, SAIC narrowed new name to Leidos," *The Washington Post*, 10 March 2013.

"Year in Review 2016: Leidos merges with Lockheed's IT business," *Washington Business Journal*, 16 December 2016.

INTERNET RESEARCH

"3D Virtual World Technology," Leidos website.

"A Peek into the Future of Incident Response," Leidos website.

"A Visionary Leader with a Lasting Legacy," Leidos website.

"Advanced Solutions," Leidos website.

"Airborne Systems Integration," Leidos website.

"Antarctic Support Contract (ASC)," Leidos website.

"Capabilities," Leidos website.

"Complex missions call for experience you can count on," Leidos website.

"Corporate Philanthropy," Leidos website.

"Dr. Beyster Tribute Video 2015," Beyster Videos/
    YouTube, published 25 February 2015.

"Environment," Leidos website.

"Health," Leidos website.

"How to Transition Into Your Civilian Career
    After Life in the Military," Leidos website.

"Investor FAQs," Leidos website.

"Managed Security," Leidos website.

"Maritime," Leidos website.

"Our History," Leidos website.

"Rankings and Awards," Leidos website.

Roger Krone bio, Leidos website.

"SAIC awarded $73 million contract by U.S. Army
    Contracting Command – New Jersey,"
    Leidos website.

"Suppliers and Small Business Relationships,"
    Leidos website.

"Survey Analysis and Area Based Editor (SABER),"
    Leidos website.

The Frederick National Lab, U.S. Department
    of Health and Human Services,
    National Institutes of Health.

"Veteran Hiring," Leidos website.

INTERVIEWS

Addison, Ann, interview by Jeffrey L. Rodengen
    and Christian Ramirez, digital recording,
    2 November 2017, Write Stuff Enterprises,
    LLC.

Anderson, Brian, interview written answers
    submitted, 2 March 2018, Write Stuff
    Enterprises, LLC.

Bannister, Patrick, interview by Christian Ramirez,
    digital recording, 26 September 2017, Write
    Stuff Enterprises, LLC.

Barbour, Sondra L., interview by Jeffrey L.
    Rodengen, digital recording, 11 July 2017,
    Write Stuff Enterprises, LLC.

Barton, Doug, interview by Christian Ramirez,
    digital recording, 23 March 2018, Write Stuff
    Enterprises, LLC.

Benjamin, Edouard, interview by Christian
    Ramirez, digital recording, 23 March 2018,
    Write Stuff Enterprises, LLC.

Beyster, Mary Ann, interview by Jeffrey L.
    Rodengen, digital recording, 29 September 2017,
    Write Stuff Enterprises, LLC.

Bidwell, Betty, interview by Jeffrey L. Rodengen
    and Christian Ramirez, digital recording,
    27 October 2017, Write Stuff Enterprises, LLC.

Brown, Michele, interview by Jeffrey L. Rodengen
    and Christian Ramirez, digital recording,
    8 August 2017, Write Stuff Enterprises, LLC.

Cantor, Jim, interview by Jeffrey L. Rodengen and
    Christian Ramirez, digital recording,
    2 November 2017, Write Stuff Enterprises, LLC.

Carr, Nevin, interview by Christian Ramirez,
    digital recording, 3 January 2018, Write Stuff
    Enterprises, LLC.

Chagnon, Michael, interview by Jeffrey L.
    Rodengen and Christian Ramirez, digital
    recording, 2 November 2017, Write Stuff
    Enterprises, LLC.

Chagnon, Michael, interview by Jeffrey L.
    Rodengen and Christian Ramirez, digital
    recording, 11 January 2018, Write Stuff
    Enterprises, LLC.

Coakley, Paul, interview written answers submit-
    ted, 21 March 2018, Write Stuff Enterprises,
    LLC.

Coogan, Michael P., interview by Jeffrey L.
    Rodengen, digital recording, 25 May 2018,
    Write Stuff Enterprises, LLC.

Cook, Rus, interview by Christian Ramirez, digital
    recording, 5 March 2018, Write Stuff
    Enterprises, LLC.

Crawford, Stuart, interview by Christian Ramirez,
    digital recording, 14 September 2017, Write
    Stuff Enterprises, LLC.

Croom, Charles E., Jr., interview by Christian
    Ramirez, digital recording, 13 February 2018,
    Write Stuff Enterprises, LLC.

Daniels, Mike, interview by Jeffrey L. Rodengen
    and Christian Ramirez, digital recording,
    27 October 2017, Write Stuff Enterprises, LLC.

Denver, Kim D., interview by Christian Ramirez, digital recording, 5 December 2017, Write Stuff Enterprises, LLC.

Fasano, Gerry, interview by Jeffrey L. Rodengen and Christian Ramirez, digital recording, 2 November 2017, Write Stuff Enterprises, LLC.

Fralick, Chuck, interview by Christian Ramirez, digital recording, 23 March 2018, Write Stuff Enterprises, LLC.

Fratamico, John J., Jr., interview by Jeffrey L. Rodengen and Christian Ramirez, digital recording, 8 August 2017, Write Stuff Enterprises, LLC.

Gemmill, Bob, interview by Jeffrey L. Rodengen, digital recording, 23 May 2018, Write Stuff Enterprises, LLC.

Grant, James, interview by Christian Ramirez, digital recording, 11 January 2018, Write Stuff Enterprises, LLC.

Harris, Walter, interview by Christian Ramirez, digital recording, 24 February 2018, Write Stuff Enterprises, LLC.

Havenstein, Walt, interview by Jeffrey L. Rodengen and Christian Ramirez, digital recording, 4 October 2017, Write Stuff Enterprises, LLC.

Heflebower, Charles "Chuck," interview by Christian Ramirez, digital recording, 15 February 2018, Write Stuff Enterprises, LLC.

Heise, Angela "Angie," interview by Jeffrey L. Rodengen and Christian Ramirez, digital recording, 2 February 2018, Write Stuff Enterprises, LLC.

Howe, Jerald S. "Jerry," Jr., interview by Jeffrey L. Rodengen and Christian Ramirez, digital recording, 2 November 2017, Write Stuff Enterprises, LLC.

Hubbly, Ravi, interview by Christian Ramirez, digital recording, 13 March 2018, Write Stuff Enterprises, LLC.

Hull, Steve, interview by Jeffrey L. Rodengen, digital recording, 8 June 2018, Write Stuff Enterprises, LLC.

Hung, Fay, interview by Christian Ramirez, digital recording, 16 March 2018, Write Stuff Enterprises, LLC.

Inman, Bobby Ray, interview by Jeffrey L. Rodengen and Christian Ramirez, digital recording, 6 November 2017, Write Stuff Enterprises, LLC.

James, Deborah Lee, interview by Jeffrey L. Rodengen, digital recording, 9 August 2017, Write Stuff Enterprises, LLC.

Jones, Anita, interview by Christian Ramirez, digital recording, 21 November 2017, Write Stuff Enterprises, LLC.

Jones, Donna, interview by Christian Ramirez, digital recording, 28 February 2018, Write Stuff Enterprises, LLC.

Jumper, John, interview by Jeffrey L. Rodengen and Christian Ramirez, digital recording, 8 August 2017, Write Stuff Enterprises, LLC.

Keller, Brian, interview by Christian Ramirez, digital recording, 16 March 2018, Write Stuff Enterprises, LLC.

Kendall, Frank, interview by Christian Ramirez, digital recording, 16 January 2018, Write Stuff Enterprises, LLC.

Koskovich, Melissa, interview by Jeffrey L. Rodengen and Christian Ramirez, digital recording, 8 August 2017, Write Stuff Enterprises, LLC.

Krampf, William, interview by Christian Ramirez, digital recording, 14 September 2017, Write Stuff Enterprises, LLC.

Kraus, Bill, interview by Christian Ramirez, digital recording, 15 February 2018, Write Stuff Enterprises, LLC.

Krone, Roger, interview by Jeffrey L. Rodengen and Christian Ramirez, digital recording, 10 August 2017, Write Stuff Enterprises, LLC.

Leiter, Tony, interview by Christian Ramirez, digital recording, 11 June 2018, Write Stuff Enterprises, LLC.

Lowy, Doug, interview by Christian Ramirez, digital recording, 8 February 2018, Write Stuff Enterprises, LLC.

Maffeo, Vince, interview by Christian Ramirez, digital recording, 31 May 2018, Write Stuff Enterprises, LLC.

Ng, Tony, interview by Christian Ramirez, digital recording, 3 January 2018, Write Stuff Enterprises, LLC.

Punaro, Arnold, interview by Jeffrey L. Rodengen and Christian Ramirez, digital recording, 8 August 2017, Write Stuff Enterprises, LLC.

Reagan, James, interview by Jeffrey L. Rodengen and Christian Ramirez, digital recording, 10 August 2016, Write Stuff Enterprises, LLC.

Reardon, Tim, interview by Jeffrey L. Rodengen and Christian Ramirez, digital recording, 1 November 2017, Write Stuff Enterprises, LLC.

Rosenberg, Robert "Rosie," interview by Jeffrey L. Rodengen and Christian Ramirez, digital recording, 9 August 2017, Write Stuff Enterprises, LLC.

Russell, Jim, interview by Jeffrey L. Rodengen, digital recording, 9 November 2017, Write Stuff Enterprises, LLC.

Scholl, Jonathan, interview by Jeffrey L. Rodengen and Christian Ramirez, digital recording, 3 November 2017, Write Stuff Enterprises, LLC.

Shiflett, James, interview by Christian Ramirez, digital recording, 2 March 2018, Write Stuff Enterprises, LLC.

Sievers, Ralph, interview by Jeffrey L. Rodengen and Christian Ramirez, digital recording, 9 August 2017, Write Stuff Enterprises, LLC.

Sopp, Mark, interview by Jeffrey L. Rodengen, digital recording, 6 July 2017, Write Stuff Enterprises, LLC.

Spikes, Gloria, interview by Christian Ramirez, digital recording, 28 September 2017, Write Stuff Enterprises, LLC.

Veldman, Ray, interview by Jeffrey L. Rodengen and Christian Ramirez, digital recording, 9 August 2017, Write Stuff Enterprises, LLC.

Wagoner, Doug, interview by Jeffrey L. Rodengen, digital recording, 22 August 2017, Write Stuff Enterprises, LLC.

Walther-Meade, George, interview by Christian Ramirez, digital recording, 27 February 2018, Write Stuff Enterprises, LLC.

Watts, Sharon, interview by Jeffrey L. Rodengen and Christian Ramirez, digital recording, 9 August 2017, Write Stuff Enterprises, LLC.

Welsh, Bettina Garcia, interview by Jeffrey L. Rodengen and Christian Ramirez, digital recording, 2 November 2017, Write Stuff Enterprises, LLC.

Zollars, Ron, interview by Jeffrey L. Rodengen and Christian Ramirez, digital recording, 27 October 2017, Write Stuff Enterprises, LLC.

PRESS RELEASES AND COMPANY DOCUMENTS

"About Leidos and Lockheed Martin IS&GS," SEC Filing, Employee FAQ, Commission File No. 001-33072.

"Air Force Association Recognizes Leidos RPA Operations Center for Outstanding Current/ Future Armed UAV Technology," PR Newswire, 14 March 2017.

Beyster, J. Robert, "Some Principles and Practices of SAI," internal company document, 6 June 1983.

"Boeing Announces the Sale of Boeing Information Services to SAIC Is Complete," PR Newswire, 23 July 1999.

"Calif-Microwave; (CMIC) California Microwave, SAIC team on Army air vehicle program," Business Wire, 11 November 1986.

"Capabilities Overview," Leidos brochure, 2015.

"Common Driver Trainer (CDT)," Leidos brochure.

"Fact sheet: As Part of the 5th Anniversary of Joining Forces, First Lady Michelle Obama and Dr. Jill Biden Announce New Private Sector Hiring and Training Commitments for Veterans and Military Spouses," White House press release, 5 May 2016.

"History of Science Applications International Corporation," Reference for Business, Copyright 2017.

"Leidos achieves perfect score in 2018 HRCF
Corporate Equality Index," Leidos media
relations release, 9 November 2017.

"Leidos Announces Closing of the Merger with
Lockheed Martin's IS&GS Business," Leidos
press release, 16 August 2016.

"Leidos Awarded Army Contract for Driver
Training Simulation Systems," PR Newswire,
8 November 2016.

"Leidos Awarded Combatant Craft Medium
MK1 Subcontract," Leidos news release,
30 April 2014.

"Leidos Awarded Contract by Defense Advanced
Research Projects Agency," Leidos news
release, 1 October 2014.

"Leidos Chairman and Chief Executive Officer
Roger Krone Named to Federal Computer
Week Federal 100," PR Newswire,
1 February 2018.

"Leidos Code of Conduct," October 2017.

"Leidos Commences Operational Testing of Highly
Autonomous Unmanned Surface Vessel,"
PR Newswire, 29 November 2016.

"Leidos Holding profit almost doubles,"
MarketWatch, 22 February 2018.

"Leidos Holdings, Inc. Reports First Quarter Fiscal
Year 2017 Results," Leidos press release,
4 May 2017.

"Leidos Holdings, Inc. Reports Fourth Quarter and
Fiscal Year 2017 Results," PR Newswire,
22 February 2018.

Leidos Holdings Q2 2017 Results Earnings Call
Transcript, 3 August 2017.

"Leidos Is Named a 2017 GCN dig IT Winner,"
PR Newswire, 23 October 2017.

"Leidos Joins Forces with IBM, Unisys, and
Verizon to Pursue the U.S. Navy's Next
Generation Enterprise Networks Re-compete
Service Management, Integration and
Transport Program," PR Newswire,
5 February 2018.

"Leidos Ranked Among LinkedIn's Top Companies
for Attracting and Retaining Talent," Leidos
press release, 18 May 2017.

"Leidos Showcases Latest Technology
Solutions at SOFIC," PR Newswire,
8 May 2014.

"Leidos to Combine with Lockheed Martin
Information Systems & Global Solutions
Business (IS&GS)," PR Newswire,
26 January 2016.

"Leidos' Skyline Air Traffic Control System
Now Operational in Korea," PR Newswire,
7 March 2017.

"Marine and Coastal Mapping," Leidos document.

"Matt Wiles Promoted to Leidos UK CEO; Roger
Krone Comments," GovCon Wire,
4 January 2018.

"NASA Awards Contract for Ground Processing of
Spaceflight Cargo," NASA contract release,
15 September 2017.

"NASA Extends SAIC Contract," Associated Press
Financial Wire, 17 September 2005.

"Navy Announces Award of Next Generation
Enterprise Network Contract," U.S. Navy news
release, 27 June 2013.

"News Release: Utilities Tap Leidos for its Smart
Grid as a Service Offering," Leidos news
release, 1 April 2014.

"News: GSA FEDSIM Awards Secure Enterprise
Network Systems, Services and Support
Contract to Leidos," Leidos press release,
12 September 2017.

"News: Leidos and Cray Inc. Announce Strategic
Alliance to Offer Multi-Level Security
Solutions," Leidos news release, 7 June 2017.

"News: Leidos Australia Partners with Bravery
Trust," Leidos Australia media relations
release, 25 July 2017.

"Oacis Agrees to Be Acquired by Science
Applications International Corporation,"
PR Newswire, 22 February 1999.

"Pinkerton and SAIC Establish Alliance to Offer
Security Solutions Against High-Tech Gangs,
Cybercriminals," Business Wire,
9 September 1996.

"Public offering would flex SAICs market muscle,"
Business Wire, 2 September 2005.

"SAIC Announces Health eTrust," PR Newswire, 10 November 1999.

"SAIC Announces Mexican Subsidiary; Opens Mexico City Office," PR Newswire, 29 November 1994.

"SAIC Announces Plan to Separate Into Two Independent, Publicly Traded Companies," PR Newswire, 30 August 2012.

"SAIC Awarded $12 Million Delivery Order to Develop U.S. Army Aviation Crew Member Simulators," Leidos news release, 2010.

"SAIC Awarded Contract by U.S. Air Force Research Laboratory (AFRL)," Leidos news release, 6 December 2012.

"SAIC Awarded Major Contract to Support the National Cancer Institute," News Release, 29 September 2008.

"SAIC Buys Out Applied Marine Technology," Associated Press Financial Wire, 18 December 2006.

"SAIC CEO Retires, Followed by BAE Systems Ex-Chief," Associated Press Financial Wire, 23 June 2009.

"SAIC Gets $160 Million Pentagon Contract," Associated Press Financial Wire, 9 December 2008.

"SAIC Gets $6.7 Million Army Night Vision Contract," Associated Press Financial Wire, 18 September 2008.

"SAIC Launches New Generation Navigation Service," PR Newswire, 9 October 2003.

"SAIC Named Successor on NASA Contract," PR Newswire, 2 January 1997.

"SAIC Plans to Offer Shares to the Public," PR Newswire, 1 September 2005.

"SAIC Receives Outstanding Prime Contractor Award," PR Newswire, 12 April 1994.

"SAIC Team to Develop Multimillion-Dollar FBI Identification System," PR Newswire, 24 August 1994.

"SAIC to Acquire Bellcore," Business Wire, 21 November 1996.

"SAIC to Acquire Software, Communications Company," PR Newswire, 17 October 1994.

"SAIC to Develop Fuel from Algae," Associated Press Financial Wire, 26 January 2009.

"SAIC to Provide Business Continuity Planning for Large Health Care Providers," PR Newswire, 7 September 1999.

"SAIC to Provide Seminars on Year 2000 Solutions," PR Newswire, 12 February 1997.

"SAIC Wins $5.2 Billion Deal From Cancer Institute," Associated Press Financial Wire, 29 September 2008.

"SAIC Wins $50 Million U.S. Navy Contract," Associated Press Financial Wire, 11 December 2007.

"SAIC Wins DOD Health Care System Information Technology Contract," PR Newswire, 22 August 1997.

"SAIC Wins NASA Contract Worth up to $69 Million," Associated Press Financial Wire, 15 December 2008.

"SAIC, Inc.'s Board of Directors Approves Spin-Off of Its Services Business," PR Newswire, 9 September 2013.

"Science Applications Gets NASA Contract," Associated Press Financial Wire, 16 October 2007.

"Soldier Monitoring System," Leidos brochure.

"Venezuelan Oil Company Selects SAIC as Partner for Information Technology Venture," PR Newswire, 16 January 1997.

U.S. Army Awards Leidos Simulation and Training Contract," PR Newswire, 18 January 2017.

U.S. Securities and Exchange Commission, Leidos Annual Report, 30 January 2015.

INDEX

*References to photographs and illustrations are given in **bold** type.*

C

J

M